I0214646

It Comes
from
the
Bible

ROBERT F. SIMMS

ALSO BY ROBERT F. SIMMS

Christianity Made Simple
The Message of Paul's Letter to the Romans

Walking the Walk, Not Just Talking the Talk: a
Commentary on James

Where Did I Come From: Your
Spiritual Nature and What it Means to You

7 Days: Seven-Day Waiting
Periods in the Bible and a Plan for
Spiritual Renewal

Ponder, Pray, Practice: 366 Daily
Devotions for Thinking Christians

Sacred Subversion

Living Life for the Highest Purpose

Ventures in Stewardship

The Challenge of Cooperation

To
my mother
who embarrasses me
with effusive praise, but
who has ever believed in me,
and at ninety-seven years of age,
still does.

It Comes

from

the

Bible

Expressions in
Modern English
from the
King James Version
of the Bible

ROBERT F. SIMMS

Copyright © 2019 by Robert F. Simms
All rights reserved. No part of this book may be reproduced or transmitted
in any form by any means, electronic or mechanical, including
photocopying, recording or by any information storage or retrieval system
without permission from the author, except for brief quotations embodied
in critical articles and reviews.

Unless otherwise marked, all scriptures are from the
King James Version of the Bible.

ISBN: 978-0-9995929-2-2
Published in the United States by
Robert F. Simms
Greer, South Carolina

Contents

Abbreviations. ii

Introduction. iii

Notes on the Entries. vi

The Listings. 9

Index of Alternate Expressions. 231

Other Phrases.. 235

Abbreviations

ASV	American Standard Version
BSB	Berean Study Bible
CEV	Contemporary English Version
CSB	Christian Standard Bible
DBT	Darby Bible Translation
ERV	English Revised Version
ESV	English Standard Version
GNT	Good News Translation
GWT	God's Word® Translation
HCSB	Holman Christian Standard Bible
ISV	International Standard Version
KJV	King James Version
NAS	New American Standard 1977
NASB	New American Standard Bible
NIV	New International Version
NLT	New Living Translation
WB	Wycliffe Bible
WBT	Webster's Bible Translation
YLT	Young's Literal Translation

Introduction

This is not the first book on the subject of words and expressions that come from the Bible, and I would think too highly of myself if I had any notion it would be the last or the best. However, I have not read any of those books, so I advise the reader that I have not drawn from any of them for my own work; I've merely seen some people's lists. It was one of those lists that gave me the idea to research the subject and write a page or two about each of a hundred or more idioms or expressions that inhabit the English language, and that many people—especially those with no Jewish or Christian experience—have no idea come from the Bible.

It may be argued, and no doubt will be, that some of the words and phrases I include in this book pre-existed English Bibles and did not enter the language altogether through the Tyndale Bible or any of the early English Bibles that came thereafter, including most notably the King James. That may be true. However, a great many words and phrases in our language that preexisted English Bibles are no longer with us due to one factor or another. One has only to read a few Shakespeare plays to find expressions and words that have to be defined for modern English speakers and readers.

As to the question of whether the entries here would have been in the English language *without* the great English Bibles produced between A.D. 1500 and 1800, I will not quibble about the matter. I think the argument for their derivation is strong enough on my side to go forward with this project, and to let the reader decide. That said, I will summarize my case with the highlights.

Obviously, the English language as it appears in the King James Version of the Bible had been developing since the 5th century with the invasion of Britain by the Angles, Saxons and Jutes coming from northern Germany. What happened with the translation of the KJV was a funneling of English through this quickly widespread and influential Bible. This funneling effect preserved and popularized idioms, expressions and terms the KJV scholars used to translate the Hebrew and Greek languages of the Bible, insuring they would continue to be in current usage in every generation thereafter as long as the King James remained influential in English cultures—which it has.

Other English works that influenced the language also contributed to modern English, notably Shakespeare's plays and sonnets. Some lists of Shakespearean phrases we use in English today number in the several dozens. One author says the Bard invented 422 words; another says 1,700, if you include making nouns into verbs, verbs into adjectives, etc.

Looking at idioms and expressions alone, however, the reader of both Shakespeare and the King James Bible (and Shakespeare died about five years after the KJV was completed), will also discover that between the two, the Bible wins the contest for the number clearly having originated there. What the English Bible, and principally the King James Bible, did was to become part of the constitution of the English culture, so to speak, a foundation stone for the continuing development not only of the language but also the concepts that underlie and inspire that language.

Consequently, when we conclude in this book that a phrase or idiom comes from the Bible, we mean particularly the King James Version of the Bible, and it will be the KJV we quote for each entry.

Barbara Bradley Hagerty, heard on NPR's "All Things Considered" on 18 Apr 2011, announced the four hundredth anniversary of the King James Version of the Bible. She spoke at length about the expressions, phrases, and simple words that we feature in this book. Hagerty interviewed David Lyle Jeffrey, a historian of biblical interpretation at Baylor

University, who told her, "These phrases have become part and parcel, then of the general usage, in the English language. We do not recognize them any longer, perhaps, as biblical unless we have a pretty good memory for the language of the KJV."

Hagerty also interviewed Gordon Campbell, a historian at the University of Leicester in England, who told her, "It's in the texture of our society rather than on the surface of it, I think. But if you trace back who we are, how we speak, how we think, many of those things have their origins in the King James Bible."[1]

This is part of our observation in this book: that English has absorbed the language of the Bible, and that speakers who have little to no knowledge of the Bible certainly don't appreciate the roots of the language, and may also fail to understand the meanings of idioms and expressions they regularly use.

The purpose of this volume is to entertain and inform. The genesis of the concept for me was a lifetime ago in a Christian upbringing, learning the words and phrases that my pastor-father used regularly. My observation of words and phrases that come from the Bible grew as I did. The catalyst for my writing this volume was seeing various lists people have made, realizing that some contained a few dozen, and some many more than I would consider definitively biblical. I decided to compose my own list, and do what I do these days more than just about anything: write. Along the way, I was, myself, entertained and further enlightened. I hope you will be, too.

---

[1]Barbara Bradley Hagerty, "Hallelujah! At Age 400, King James Bible Still Reigns" 18 Apr 2011 (https://www.npr.org/2011/04/18/135437890/king-james-bible-now-400-still-echoes-voice-of-god) Accessed 17 Jan 2019.

Notes on the Entries

■ Entries are alphabetical. Most initial articles and some prepositions have been deleted so that the first word is the most important, as in "Blind leading the blind," where "the," almost always precedes the first "blind," but is omitted here. Otherwise, you'd be searching through quite a few "the's" to find what you're looking for. Exceptions are where the initial "throwaway" word is nothing of the kind. If you can't find what you're looking for, omit an initial preposition or article. If that doesn't work, go to the list in the back of words and expressions not included for discussion. If you still can't find it, I missed one! Write me at *rfsimms@charter.net*.

■ Unless otherwise stated, quotations of Bible verses are from the King James Version (KJV).

■ Some quotations cited as in the King James Version actually exist in earlier versions of the Bible, such as the Coverdale Bible (1535) or others. The fact that most people don't have quick access to these more antiquated versions is the reason I have chosen to refer to the KJV.

■ Some modern versions of Bible phrases achieved their present form very soon after the Bible books were written, and word order or other changes were adopted. For instance, the word "prodigal" nowhere appears in the English version of the Parable of the Prodigal Son. The word is merely descriptive of the son who took his inheritance early and wasted it all in "riotous living" in a far country. In the entries included in this book, the source is not in doubt, though the wording of the modern phrases may not be exactly as they appear in the Bible, whether English versions or the original languages.

■ Readers may try to find phrases that we have not included here, and many of these will be biblical phrases that are almost never used except by Jews or Christians in *quoting* the Bible. Thus, they really are not everyday English. "Bread of life,"

"Blessed are the peacemakers," "Kingdom of heaven," and "Our daily bread" are examples. Other phrases are found in titles of songs, books and plays, etc. but rarely in conversation or writing except to refer to these artistic works. At the back of the book is a short list of these more-or-less proprietary phrases.

■ Footnotes are sometimes in standard form according to some footnote style, but not always the same one, alas. The problem in this size book is the amount of space footnotes take up and the almost incredible length that Internet addresses can be. I copied one that was fifteen lines long. Ultimately I didn't include the source at all. We adjudged that it wasn't always critical to list the entire URL when we had given the basic location, author, and other information. Some notes are inline, too, especially when we included multiple quotes on the same page and would have filled up half the page with footnote citations. That always makes a page look too "scholarly" to me, and I felt it would have been off-putting to the reader. We could have made footnotes into endnotes and kept the text pages cleaner, but our experience with notes is that when a reader wants to read one, he doesn't want to go to the back and find it: he wants it at the bottom of the page. So we minimized where possible. In some instances we simply claim the fair usage clause of the copyright law. So there.

The Listings

All things to all men

This phrase is not entirely idiomatic, though we'll refer to It that way. Anyone might come up with it naturally to express the idea inherent in it. But as a well known phrase it came into English through the translation of a statement by Paul the Apostle:

1 Corinthians 9:22 "I have become all things to all men, that I might by all means save some."

In 2016 the *New York Post* used the "people" instead of "men" version of this idiom in 2016 to recommend to Donald Trump that he campaign for a broader electorate. *USA Today* employed "all things to all people" in commenting on the need of small colleges to specialize.

The modern, secular usage usually implies a negative thought. "People pleasers," those mildly tortured souls who derive their sense of self worth by securing the approval of others, sometimes critique themselves with the phrase.

In Paul's usage, however, the phrase was a summary of his method of evangelism. His broader comment in verses 19-23 of 1 Corinthians 9 begins with this statement: " For though I am free from all men, I have made myself a servant to all, that I might win the more." He assured his readers that he was not some sort of slave to the approval of others; rather, he adapted himself to circumstances to reach other people with the gospel. In colloquial English we might say he "played up" his identity as a Jew in order to reach Jews, and accentuated his Gentile connection of being a Roman citizen to reach Gentiles, etc.

Amen to that

The Bible word "amen" comes from both the Greek in which the New Testament and Old Testament Septuagint were written and the Hebrew of the Old Testament, in which the word was *aleph mem nun*.[2] It meant "truth" or "faithful" or "reliable." The earliest use of the word in English Bibles is in the Torah:

Num.5:22 "And this water that causeth the curse shall go into thy bowels, to make thy belly to swell, and thy thigh to rot: And the woman shall say, Amen, amen."

A suspected sorceress was compelled to say "true, true," to the priest's charges.

The New Testament usage of "Amen" is no doubt more persuasive in its being part of everyday English (though much more pervasive in Christian circles). "Amen to that" has the closely related sense of, "I agree wholeheartedly." Or, as it is often said mostly in the black community, "True dat."

An article in *M/C Journal* concerned the frequent use of the "Amen break," a drum sequence originally performed by the Winstons in 1969 on a B-side recording called, "Amen, Brother." The title of the article, "Amen to that."[3]

A Facebook post about the annual Sturgis Motorcycle Rally said, "Many people go to church to feel spiritual. I get on my bike to cleanse my soul. All the things in life that bother me fade away mile by mile." An anonymous person commented, "Amen to that." The author can relate.

---

[2]The earliest Hebrew didn't contain vowels. The Masoretes later contributed "pointed" letters, indications of the accepted vowel sounds.
[3]Collins, Steve. "Amen to That: Sampling and Adapting the Past." M/C Journal 10.2 (2007). <http://journal.media-culture.org.au/0705/09-collins.php>.

Apple of his eye

This idiom is quite old in English. It predates any English translation of the Bible, being found in a ninth century (A.D.) work of King Aelfred the Great of Wessex, later in Shakespeare (*A Midsummer Night's Dream*), and other places. Its earliest instance in the Bible is in the Pentateuch, and then in the Psalms and Proverbs:

Deuteronomy 32:10 "...he guarded him as the apple of his eye."

Psalm 17:8 "Keep me as the apple of the eye, hide me under the shadow of thy wings."

Proverbs 7:2 "Keep my commandments, and live; and my law as the apple of thine eye."

The Hebrew word translated "apple" is the same in every instance. But it isn't the same word used in the Hebrew Bible to refer to the fruit of the apple tree. Actually, in this sense "apple" appears in the Bible in naming the apple tree (Song of Solomon 2:3, 8:5, Joel 1:12), and it's a different Hebrew word.

The fact is, when the English translators first looked at the Hebrew expression, "*kə-i-so-wn-bat-ayin*" (transliteration), they drew on preexisting English terminology for the part of the eye we know today as the iris. In the sixteenth century, the English called it the apple of the eye. It was round and dark. It reminded them of an apple, we suppose. At any rate, the job of translators is to find the best word or combination of words in the target language to represent the meaning of the original, and "apple of the eye" was it.

While "iris" is the denotation, the connotation of the "apple" part of the eye is something precious and worthy of guarding and protecting—thus Deuteronomy 32:10. Lamentations 2:18

uses another Hebrew word to designate the iris and has a similar sense of something to protect.

The apple of one's eye is something or someone held dear more than anything or anyone else. The phrase is almost never used to refer to a body part, even the eye itself. Its most common reference is to someone the speaker loves, such as a spouse or only child. We hope the speaker would not tell one child she was the apple of his eye and leave another child to wonder if he's loved at all!

Armageddon

This evocative word has been used liberally by the arts community. Among many other instances, it was a 1963 novel by Leon Uris, and a 1998 film starring Bruce Willis. The word comes from the last book of the Bible.

Revelation 16:16 "And he gathered them together into a place called in the Hebrew tongue Armageddon."

The sixth of seven angels appearing to bring about terrible events in the days of the second coming of Jesus Christ is to bring the kings of the earth to the valley of Megiddo, the valley below *har-megiddo*, thus Armageddon. Napolean, it is said, stood on the slopes of Megiddo and pronounced the valley the most perfect spot on earth for a battle.

Nuclear war, the prospect of which inspires unsurpassed fear, is often referred to as Armageddon. In spite of that, game creators have come up with a role-playing game called "Armageddon." Perhaps they were just whistling in the dark.

The World Chess Championship also has a final round, played only if one of the chess grandmasters cannot take a decisive win before the clock runs out. The deciding round is played under rules designed to force a win for one or the other. It's called—you guessed it—Armageddon. We're getting far afield, here.

But the paltriest understanding the author has heard of the biblical term was uttered by U.S. House Leader Nancy Pelosi, about the health care bill before it in December 2017. Said Pelosi irresponsibly, "The debate on healthcare is like death. This is Armageddon."

It was nothing of the sort, of course; nor was the asteroid Bruce Willis saved the world from, as terrible as such an event would be if it were to occur.

Ashes to ashes, dust to dust

Anyone who has been to a few funerals has probably heard the expression, "ashes to ashes, dust to dust." It's somber. It's humbling. Sometimes it's downright depressing. But it's a fact of humanity, and yes, at least part of it comes from the Bible.

The entire phrase comes from the Anglican Common Book of Prayer, the burial service: "We therefore commit his/her body to the ground/its final resting-place; earth to earth, ashes to ashes, dust to dust" (etc.).

"Dust to dust" comes from early in the Bible:

Genesis 3:19 "For dust thou art, and to dust thou shalt return."

A similar verse appears later in a likely work of Solomon:

Ecclesiastes 12:7 "Then shall the dust return to the earth as it was: and the spirit shall return unto God who gave it."

From these verses Freemasonry constructed its funeral lament, on which they comment: "This last portion of the Masonic degree verse refers to "ashes to ashes, dust to dust", which are still the words voiced when we inter (bury) the dead."[4]

Dozens and dozens of artistic works have drawn titles from one or the other part of this phrase. Apparently, most people soberly realize that "all we are is dust in the wind."[5]

---

[4]Masonic Lodge of Education, Available at *https://www.masonic-lodge-of-education.com/masonic-degree-verse.html*, the Internet, Accessed 12/20/2018.

[5]Kerry Livgren, "Dust in the Wind," of the rock band Kansas, on "Point of Know Return," (Legacy Recordings, 1977).

At wits' end

These days, "wit" generally means "sense of humor." The plural "wits," however, means mental sharpness or aptitude. We retain that sense in the expression "to keep one's wits about him."

In the days of King James, "wit" meant knowledge. To be at one's wit's end, therefore, meant to be at the end of one's knowledge, to be unable to figure out what to do. The phrase still means that today.

Psalm 107:27 "They reel to and fro, and stagger like a drunken man, and are at their wits' end."

George Gordon Lord Byron famously said of a Cardinal acquaintance, "The Cardinal is at his wit's end; it is true that he had not far to go."

The reader will notice that in this entry the apostrophe in "wits'" is after the "s," as it is in the King James Version. In Byron's remark, he placed the apostrophe before the "s." Grammarist, a highly regarded grammar website, says that since we say "I'm at the end of my wits," using the plural, we should say "my wits' end." It makes sense.

An online description of an episode of the Simi Sara radio program describes it this way: "Owners in a North Vancouver townhouse complex say they are at their wit's end with an owner who is running their townhouse as an unlicensed and illegal hostel."

The writer himself is at his wits' end trying to get people, when they say "short lived," to pronounce the vowel in "lived" as in "dived," rather than as in "give." In the expression, "lived" is derived from the noun "life" rather than the verb "to live." How would you say, "My cat is nine-lived"?

Baptism of fire

The writer has long spoken of his first career position after grad school as his trial by fire. A closely related expression is this current entry. It comes from the Bible:

Matthew 3:11 "...he that cometh after me is mightier than I, whose shoes I am not worthy to bear: he shall baptize you with the Holy Ghost, and with fire."

John the Baptist baptized with water, but he was only paving the way for Jesus. The baptism Jesus would perform, which would take place after his passion, resurrection and ascension, would be with the Holy Spirit and fire. The fire, of course, was figurative. It represented the Spirit's purification and power. Interestingly, when this baptism of the disciples took place at Pentecost, the Spirit let his presence be known with a vision of tongues of fire appearing above their heads.

A baptism by fire continues to express the idea of an initial experience in any endeavor that brings home bluntly the inherent challenge of it and that subjects the initiate to an especially strong dose of what his undertaking is about.

Wilfried Martens described his first EPP Congress in 1990 after his accession to the presidency of the European People's Party as his baptism by fire. It was the first such congress after the fall of the Berlin wall and was an administrative hardship for him.

Far less significant was the baptism by fire Zack Hess, an LSU pitcher, said a particularly tough baseball game was. But John Hughes, a marine and survivor of Pearl Harbor, had a literal baptism by fire. He was ashore but ran to the airfield in a desperate attempt to help repel the Japanese attack. Hoo-rah!

Be fruitful and multiply

Admittedly, this phrase is most often heard in a religious context as a quotation from the first book of the Bible:

Genesis 9:1 "God blessed Noah and his sons, and said unto them, Be fruitful, and multiply, and replenish the earth."

Now and then someone will use the phrase in another context. An abstract of an article in a U.S. National Library of Medicine publication referred to "gene amplification inducing pathogen resistance" as being fruitful and multiplying.[6] Who knew? And *Science News* likens "matter waves" to a non-biological example of being fruitful and multiplying.[7]

In Christianity the phrase is applied to reproduction other than biological, such as evangelism and church planting.[8]

The Preschool at Temple Shalom encourages its supporters to "be fruitful and multiply our school resources." Their goal is $1,000. To date they've gotten nothing. Maybe the parents have the products of their own multiplication to supply.[9]

Not everyone thinks the twice-given biblical commandment is a good idea. Quite a few non-religious (and some religious) sources lambast any encouragement to have children in this day and time, because of frantic concern of overpopulation. The warning seems to be ignored by most newlyweds.

---

[6]C. Peterhansel, "Be Fruitful and Multiply..." (*Trends in Plant Science,* June 10, 2005); Available from https://www.ncbi.nlm.nih.gov/pubmed/15949756, the Internet.

[7]Peter Weiss, "Matter Waves: Be Fruitful and Multiply," (*Science News,* May 31, 2002); Available from *https://www.sciencenews.org/article/matter-waves-be-fruitful-and-multiply*; the Internet.

[8]See David Reagan, "Be Fruitful and Multiply: The Missing Ministry in Today's Churches" (*http://www.learnthebible.org*).

[9](https://www.farmraiser.com/campaigns/be-fruitful-and-multiply-our-school-resources/market)

Bear fruit

We could argue that to bear fruit is too general as a phrase in any language for us to claim it comes from the Bible. But its appearance in the English language is strongly tied to the biblical idea. It shows up in the Bible some thirty times, usually in the figurative sense, such as in Jesus' admonition:

John 15:2 "Every branch in me that beareth not fruit he taketh away: and every branch that beareth fruit, he purgeth it, that it may bring forth more fruit."

Jesus drew on a solid history of the use of the phrase (in Aramaic and previously in Hebrew) to represent godly people living godly lives:

Ezekiel 17:23 "In the mountain of the height of Israel will I plant it: and it shall bring forth boughs, and bear fruit, and be a goodly cedar: and under it shall dwell all fowl of every wing; in the shadow of the branches thereof shall they dwell."

A student expresses hope that his studying abroad will bear fruit. A diplomat hopes aloud that a Syrian-Saudi effort to calm a developing crisis in Lebanon will bear fruit. Some people thought that in spite of President Obama's announcement of what eventually became DACA (The Deferred Action for Childhood Arrivals program), it was doubtful Congress's efforts would bear fruit.[10]

It did, of course, but we still need to address the *root*, not just the *fruit* of the illegal immigration problem.

---

[10]Vauhini Vara, "The Immigrants excluded by Obama's new plan," (<*https://www.lccr.com/newsroom/immigrants-excluded-obamas-new-plan/*>)

Beat swords into ploughshares

Isaiah the prophet looked far into the future and under the inspiration of the Spirit this is what he saw:

Isaiah 2:4 "And he shall judge among the nations, and shall rebuke many people: and they shall beat their swords into plowshares, and their spears into pruninghooks: nation shall not lift up sword against nation, neither shall they learn war any more."

The words of Micah 4:3 are nearly identical. The prophets saw a lot of war. The empires of Assyria and Babylon had wreaked great havoc on surrounding nations in the ancient world, including Israel and Judah. Conquering armies had a bad habit of taking substantial portions of conquered populations back to the homeland to be slaves. Not nice.

Conquerors seemed to like war—the conquered, not so much. So, the dream and prayer of the people of Israel as well as the perennially overrun and defeated peoples of diminutive nations who were no match for the marauding empires, was that the time would come when wars would cease. Beat those swords into plows and do something constructive and helpful with them!

Like "Be fruitful and multiply," "Swords into plowshares" is found largely in a religious context in English. Outside of church and synagogue, it usually crops up in somebody's praise or damnation of scriptural exhortation, or in the title of a sculpture at the U.N. And it's essentially uncontroversial. Very few people are willing to go on record as opposing the dream that one day all the energy humanity now expends on war and self defense will be unnecessary, and life may be lived in peace and productivity.

Behemoth

Lots of things have been described by the word "behomoth:" the T-43 heavy tank partly designed by Chrysler; the Chrysler Corporation itself;[11] the defense budget of the United States (the proposed budget for 2018 was $639.1 billion); the State Hermitage Museum in St. Petersburg, Russia; a storm on Saturn identified by NASA; the Amazon Corporation, according mainly to its critics, but the title is apt. As the King of Siam said in The King and I, "Etcetera, etcetera."

The word "behemoth" comes from the Bible (naturally).

Job 40:15-18 "Behold now behemoth, which I made with thee; he eateth grass as an ox. Lo now, his strength is in his loins, and his force is in the navel of his belly. He moveth his tail like a cedar: the sinews of his stones are wrapped together. His bones are as strong pieces of brass; his bones are like bars of iron."

The description goes on for another six verses. Clearly the beast was huge and impressive. Some people believe it was a dinosaur. Some think it was whatever now inhabits Loch Ness. Regardless, it was *big*, really *big*.

Thus, a behemoth is anything startling or remarkable for its size, and the phrase is broadly used (as above) to refer to not only living things but also physical structures, mechanical objects (such as the Bucyrus RH400, the world's largest hydraulic shovel), and organizations.

There's even a fruit that has been described as a behemoth, the SteakHouse Tomato (actually, the tomato is a fruit, botanically speaking). This tomato is the size of a small pumpkin. You can buy the seeds from Burpee.

---

[11]Dieter Zetsche, who said, "We think a behemoth of this size is just not responsible."

Better to give than to receive

It's interesting, and altogether understandable, that secular society is all too eager to adopt and liberally use idioms and figures of speech that come from the Bible as long as they aren't direct expressions of Bible teachings: those they leave to the religious community.

It's difficult to divorce oneself entirely from the biblical origin of this saying, however, because of the fact that Jesus himself said it. Paul gave us the quote in a speech delivered to the elders of the church at Ephesus:

Acts 20:35 "...remember the words of the Lord Jesus, how he said, It is more blessed to give than to receive."

I say it's *difficult* to pretend the saying isn't a Bible teaching, but it's not impossible. And, the teaching has been subjected to the same kind of criticism as many other principles that come from the Bible. "Leadership Freak," the blogosphere business of Dan Rockwell, published an article by Jesse Lyn Stoner of Seapoint Center for Collaborative Leadership, in which Stoner first misquotes Jesus thusly: "It is better to give than to receive." Then he casts doubt on the altered saying: "It's so ingrained in our culture, we don't even question it. ...It's easier to give than to receive, but not necessarily better. ...What's important is knowing *when* to give and *when* to receive."[12]

James Randerson in *The Guardian* strips the saying from its source, also misquotes it, and calls it simply "an old adage."[13]

---

[12]Jesse Lyn Stoner, "It's Better to Give than to Receive, and Other Lies" (*Leadership Freak*, Dec. 19, 2011) Available from *https://leadershipfreak.blog/2011/12/19/its-better-to-give-than-receive-and-other-lies/*, the Internet; Accessed 12/20/2018.

[13]James Randerson, "The Path to Happiness" (*The Guardian*, March 20, 2008) Available from *https://www.theguardian.com/science/2008/mar/21/medicalresearch.usa*.

Bite the dust

As everyone who ever watched cowboy movies and television shows knows, to bite the dust is to die, to be killed, or in the metaphorical sense, to fail miserably.

Its ultimate origin is the Psalms:

Psalm 72:9 "They that dwell in the wilderness shall bow before him; and his enemies shall lick the dust."

The Scottish author Tobias Smollett adapted the older phrase in his *Adventures of Gil Blas of Santillane* (1750) and gave us the present form, with "bite."

Etymologists who know their stuff, however, will point to Homer's, *The Iliad*. Thirty years before Smollett's work, Alexander Pope had rendered a phrase in *The Iliad* as "bite the ground." Then in 1898, Samuel Butler translated *The Iliad* and rendered the same passage, one of Agamemnon's prayers, this way: "Grant that my sword may pierce the shirt of Hector about his heart, and that full many of his comrades may bite the dust as they fall dying round him." The Iliad was written about 800 B.C. according to some authorities, around 700 B.C. according to others. The casual etymologist will argue that long before the English Bible or Tobias Smollett, Homer wrote of people biting the dust—in Greek, of course.

Not so fast. The Greek text of the Iliad varies according to the source, but is essentially the same. In Thomas Clark's Interlinear Iliad (1888)[14], the Greek words uttered by Agamemnon are rendered, "him headlong (prostrate) in (the) dust may lay hold of (the) earth with (the) teeth." Samuel Butler's translation was not exact. In fact, he compressed and reinterpreted the original language and rendered it through

---

[14]Thomas Clark, *The Iliad of Homer, with an Interlinear Translation* (David McKay Company, Inc., New York, 1888), 85.

the "paraphrase" method. He used the idiom, "bite the dust," to render the less elegant Greek. He didn't invent the expression: it predated him. Butler got the idiom from Smollett and everyone else who had been using it for more than a hundred years, not from the Iliad, which he didn't render word-for-word.

We're back to the question of the ultimate origin of the phrase. Even if the Iliad had come close to "bite the dust," it isn't as old as Psalm 72. The Iliad may date as early as 800 B.C., but the likely date of Psalm 72 is around 1015 B.C. Expressing death with the imagery of the human mouth eating the dust of the earth may have even earlier roots, but we don't know of them. After the Psalm was composed, more than two hundred years went by, during which the Hebrew Scriptures were copied, recopied and made their way into surrounding lands as Jews took them there. It seems safe to say that the ultimate source of "bite the dust" is the Bible.

Blind leading the blind

Isaiah the prophet lived somewhere between 760 and 686 B.C., give or take a few years on either end. In what is now referred to sometimes as Deutero-Isaiah or Second Isaiah, he wrote that "Israel's watchmen are blind." A blind watchman is pretty much useless. By the time of Jesus some 700 years later, the Hebrew language and then Aramaic contained sayings featuring the wisdom of this obvious logic.

Hebrew traditions are not the only ones featuring the imagery of blind people attempting to lead other blind people. The Upanishads, Buddhist writings, Horace and Sextus Empiricus all include similar sayings. These sources developed with relative independence. There can be no doubt, however, that the source for the specific form of the idiom in English is the Bible, which had powerful, formative force upon our language during early English history.

Two verses in the New Testament provide the source:

Matthew 15:13-14 "Let them alone: they be blind leaders of the blind. And if the blind lead the blind, both shall fall into the ditch."

Luke 6:39 "And he spake a parable unto them, Can the blind lead the blind? shall they not both fall into the ditch?"

Someone on an Internet language site asked for help: "I'm looking for an alternative to the blind leading the blind that won't be offensive to anyone." The 21st century preoccupation with being offended at everything would rid the culture of some of its most useful idioms, this one included. There should be nothing offensive about it. The author has led blind persons in various situations—they request it. Most completely unsighted people welcome help in unfamiliar places, usually wanting to simply place their hand under the elbow of their sighted guide. They aren't offended at all by being offered assistance—guidance—and I'm quite certain they would recognize the folly of accepting help from someone who could no more see than they could, especially if that person had no more knowledge of where he was.

Obviously, the expression "blind leading the blind" means someone attempting to lead or instruct another person in a subject about which he has inadequate knowledge or none at all.

Peter Layton produces masterpieces of glasswork in London. He was trained in ceramics, but "learnt glassblowing by attending a summer workshop at the University of Iowa in the 1960s, where he was teaching pottery." Layton said, "It was a case of the blind leading the blind in the early days, with the teachers knowing little more than the students."[15]

---

[15]Nathan Brooker, "Christmas Baubles" Financial Times 28 Nov 2014 (https://www.ft.com/content/3187c7ae-719c-11e4-b178-00144feabdc0)

Born again

It's defensible to say this phrase didn't really enter the *general* vernacular—and when it did, almost exclusively in American English—until the presidential candidacy of Jimmy Carter in 1978. Since then the concept has been lauded and ridiculed, reverenced and lampooned. It was said first to Nicodemus, a Pharisee and member of the Jewish Sanhedrin intensely interested in what Jesus was teaching:

John 3:3 - "Jesus answered and said unto him, Verily, verily, I say unto thee, Except a man be born again, he cannot see the kingdom of God."

The accepted meaning for most of our culture is somewhat generic. Merriam-Webster (my go-to dictionary) says that "born again" means "of, relating to, or being a usually Christian person who has made a renewed or confirmed commitment of faith especially after an intense religious experience." I suspect Jesus would have smiled gently and corrected M-W. His meaning, as explained and repeated throughout the New Testament, is that a human spirit is regenerated by the entrance and work of the Holy Spirit, upon one's turning in repentance and faith to Jesus Christ as Son of God and Savior. Put succinctly from another perspective, it means to have a datable conversion to Christ.

Most Christians would probably not mind the somewhat secular use of the term, however, as long as it's applied judiciously. When used, non-Christians naturally don't make any reference to seeing the kingdom of God, which Jesus said was conditioned upon being born again.

Some usage of the phrase would be less welcome to Christians, but that doesn't seem to matter. Anthony Kronman's book, *Confessions of a Born-Again Pagan*, "leads its readers away from the inscrutable Creator of the Abrahamic religions toward a God whose inexhaustible and everlasting presence is that of the world itself." Kronman calls this religious faith "the born-again paganism on which modern science, art, and politics all vitally depend."[16] In this sense, born again means nothing more than a return to a conviction, with intensified zeal.

On the other, mostly positive, side you can find in print a *Born Again Runner* (a book), Born Again the band, a born again steak restaurant chain (Gauchos), a wholly born again country (Japan), and a born again car (Ford Bronco). There's a born again fighter (Derek Chisora), born again bodies (they lost weight), and born again television programs ("Last Man Standing"). People on the political right have sometimes been referred to as born again conservatives.

About the best use of the concept, reworded slightly for his particular use, was at the end of Abraham Lincoln's Gettysburg Address:

> …We here highly resolve that these dead shall not have died in vain—that this nation, under God, shall have a new birth of freedom, and that government of the people, by the people, for the people, shall not perish from the earth.

---

[16] Anthony T. Kronman, in his description of *Confessions of a Born Again Pagan*, on *https://yalebooks.yale.edu/book/9780300208535/confessions-born-again-pagan*, The Internet.

Bottomless pit

Most mothers have described a ravenous teenager as a bottomless pit. There is an age, when hormones and metabolism kick in at a furious pace, that teens become eating machines. They seemingly cannot be filled. Yet they don't seem to become fat—a phenomenon of youth of which older adults are bitterly envious.

The phrase originates in Revelation:

Revelation 9:1 "And the fifth angel sounded, and I saw a star fall from heaven unto the earth: and to him was given the key of the bottomless pit."

The term "Abyss" is also applied (Revelation 9:2, Luke 8:31, etc.). The biblical term refers to a phenomenon somewhere in creation where Satan and his angels will be confined for eternity.

The phrase has fairly frequent usage today, especially in fascinating speculation about features of the earth. A crater in Siberia has scientists wondering whether it has any bottom. They think it may have been the product of the Tunguska explosion in 1908. Of course, if it were truly bottomless, there would be a matching hole on the other side of the globe, and as yet no one has threaded anything through it.

We've remarked in this book how the medical science world has often used biblical phrases (See: Fat of the land). What terms they eschew, the world of rock music or gaming has appropriated, especially the terminology of disaster and judgment. A rock band from Chicago named itself "Bottomless Pit." An experimental, hip-hop band called Death Grips produced an album by the name "Bottomless Pit." And a hazard in platforming video games is called a bottomless pit, as is a spell in World of Warcraft.

Bread upon the waters

Rudyard Kipling wrote a short story published in 1895 titled *Bread Upon the Waters,* about a ship's engineer who attempts to prevent accidents by reducing liner speed and is fired by his employer. But later he is rewarded by the same company for salvaging one of its ships abandoned at sea.[17]

The fuller phrase, comes from the Bible (are you surprised?):

Ecclesiastes 11:1 "Cast thy bread upon the waters: for thou shalt find it after many days."

Some sources say the principle use of the saying in today's English means doing something kind without expecting anything in return. If that is, indeed, the prevailing use, it's inconsistent with the scripture the phrase comes from, since Ecclesiastes promises a return, whether or not it is in kind.

Literal, baked bread is not meant. Anyone who has ever fed ducks in a pond with loaf bread knows that it turns to mush in two seconds. It won't ever come back to you. In Ecclesiastes the word actually means "grain." The NIV translates the choppy Hebrew this way: "Ship your grain across the sea; after many days you may receive a return." The next verse clarifies that what is envisioned is investment. It is therefore an admonition to use the resources you have in the wisest manner for the greatest return. Verse 2, in fact, specifically says invest in multiple ventures because you don't know what will happen to just one. In other words, Ecclesiastes 11:1-2 is about diversifying your portfolio!

It's often the case that investment language in the Bible has a spiritual application regarding non-monetary things.

---

[17]The story eerily presages, at this point, the sinking of Titanic, seventeen years later, which attempted to break records crossing the North Atlantic on its maiden voyage, and was unable to steer clear of an iceberg spotted too late.

Investment is a common metaphor, especially in the teachings of Jesus, for good stewardship of everything you have in this life. Jesus' teaching featured a similar principle: "Give, and it shall be given unto you; good measure, pressed down, and shaken together, and running over, shall men give into your bosom. For with the same measure that ye mete withal it shall be measured to you again" (Luke 6:38). And to the exact point of Ecclesiastes, Jesus taught in his parable of the pounds that those whose invest well will be rewarded:

> Then came the first, saying, Lord, thy pound hath gained ten pounds. And he said unto him, Well, thou good servant: because thou hast been faithful in a very little, have thou authority over ten cities …For I say unto you, That unto every one which hath shall be given; and from him that hath not, even that he hath shall be taken away from him (Luke 19:16-17, 26).

"Cast thy bread upon the waters," therefore *should* mean the same thing today, though often it doesn't. Usually it does when handled rightly by Bible teachers.

Mike Scott, an Arizona pastor who hosts a regional and international television program of Bible teaching, says, "I believe that this entire context is a discussion of benevolence. The encouragement here is to be a benevolent person, because one never knows when he might be in need of benevolence himself."[18] This is perhaps the most common interpretation, and gets at the spiritual principle, even if it doesn't include the financial wisdom inherent in the verse.

---

[18]Mike Scott, "What does the expression, 'Cast your bread upon many waters' in Ecc. 11:1 mean?" *(http://www.scripturessay.com/what-does-the-expression-cast-your-bread-on-many-waters-in-ecc-111-mean/)* The Internet; Accessed 12/21/2018.

Broken heart

Some sources put the origin of the English form of this phrase around A.D. 1300. Other sources say it's at least 3,000 years old—obviously in other languages. We're concerned here with English, and again, the profound influence of the Bible on the formation of modern English leads us to the Psalms:

Psalm 34:18 "The LORD is nigh unto them that are of a broken heart; and saveth such as be of a contrite spirit."

The oldest meaning of the phrase in English is one that is retained in modern English mostly, if not almost exclusively, in religious communities, where it is a synonym for being deeply sorrowful for sin. Usually the condition is produced by powerful experiences that humble a person and make him realize his desperate need of forgiveness and the grace of God.

Two other meanings are common in English, however, especially in the verb form, "to break one's heart." One of those meanings is, "deeply moved," especially to compassion and empathy: "To see animals mistreated like this—it just breaks your heart and you have to do something."

The other is, of course, in the romantic setting, where it means hopes are dashed and emotions are brought to a nadir of anguish: "He broke my heart. I'm not sure I'll ever love again."

Interestingly, the medical world uses the phrase, too. It's officially called takotsubo cardiomyopathy or stress-induced cardiomyopathy. The "tako-tsubo" descriptor is a Japanese word for a basket used catch octopi (what most of us would call octopuses). The left ventricle of the heart reminds the Japanese of this basket, apparently, and when they were looking for a term to call a syndrome involving temporary heart failure due to emotional stress, they applied this word. In English speaking countries the more colloquial term is "broken heart syndrome."

It sounds like what it is. Great emotional distress may generate psychosomatic or psychogenic changes in the body resulting in actual heart failure. People can, in fact, die from a broken heart.

But then, we all knew that. Hundreds of books stretching back through centuries tell us of people who died of a broken heart. Pope Paschal II was described as having succumbed to a broken heart, as was Henry of England.[19] Jane Goodall, the famous primatologist, believed that a chimpanzee named Flint had died of a broken heart after his sister Flame died.[20] More lately, Debbie Reynolds is believed widely to have died of a broken heart. Debbie was the mother of Carrie Fisher, best known as Princess Leia in *Star Wars*. In later years in particular, mother and daughter were inseparable. Debbie passed away quite unexpectedly only one day after daughter Carrie died following a heart attack.

---

[19]John W. Parker, *A History of Popery* (London, John W. Parker, West Strand, 1838) 66.
[20]Frederic M. Menger, "Thin Bone Vault, The: The Origin Of Human Intelligence," *World Scientific* (Feb 11, 2009) 214.

Brother's keeper

President Obama liked to go around campaigning (even after he was elected), telling people that we are our brother's keeper. He did this to justify taxing Americans more heavily and distributing the proceeds to the "entitled" and to foreign countries. On another front, in 2014 he launched a foundation called My Brother's Keeper "to address persistent opportunity gaps facing boys and young men of color and to ensure all youth can reach their full potential."[21] He liked the idea of basing his large scale charitable acts (meaning the increased burden on taxpayers) on what he purported to be scriptural principles.

It took David Kaczynski 18 years to piece together the clues that mounted over that time that his brother Ted was the Unibomber. But when he finally did in 1996, he went to the FBI in a sobering inverse of being his brother's keeper. In doing so, he was more positively looking after the well being of who knows how many additional victims his mentally ill brother might have killed.

And any time a newspaper or magazine does an article on brothers where one helps the other, "My Brother's Keeper" is likely to be in the title.

The phrase comes from the Bible, but the question is whether it means what people *use* it to mean these days.

Genesis 4:9 "And the LORD said unto Cain, Where is Abel thy brother? And he said, I know not: Am I my brother's keeper?"

Cain was jealous of Abel because God approved of Abel's sacrifice of an animal but didn't "have regard" for Cain's basket of fruit and veggies. Cain waited until they were alone

---

[21]*https://www.obama.org/mbka/*, The Internet.

and then killed his brother. When the Lord asked Cain where Abel was, Cain's answer was a denial of responsibility for keeping tabs on his brother. It's even defensible to say that Cain was asking a rhetorical question and that he *wasn't*, in fact, his brother's keeper. Cain wasn't claiming that he was under no obligation to love his brother and care about his welfare. He was simply denying that he was personally responsible for knowing where his brother was and what he was doing at all hours of the day.

Perhaps because we read too much into the sarcasm of Cain, we have a tendency to enlarge the opposite of his question into an overstatement, namely that we are our brother's keeper. Are we?

The perceived *opposite* of *not* being our brother's keeper is claimed by presidents, charities, social activists and moralists to be an all encompassing commitment by each of us to the happiness, safety and welfare of everyone else.

Methinks that's a wee bit of exaggeration. Nevertheless, "my brother's keeper" has come into English mostly sans "Am I," making it a general purpose idiom plied by one group of people to prompt, in another group, a sense of guilt and responsibility.

Sometimes it works.

Busybodies

Everybody knows a busybody, one of those people who concern themselves with nothing so much as *your* business. "Busybody" existed in the English of Queen Elizabeth I and King James, of course, but it might not have survived their era and made it into modern English had it not been for its use in the works of the Apostle Paul, as translated in the KJV:

2 Thessalonians 3:11 "For we hear that there are some which walk among you disorderly, working not at all, but are busybodies."

1 Timothy 5:13 "And withal they learn to be idle, wandering about from house to house; and not only idle, but tattlers also and busybodies, speaking things which they ought not."

The CEV renders the last phrase of the previous verse, which more or less defines the word "busybody," as "talking about things that are none of their business." A busybody is likely to begin a conspiratorial query with, "Well, you know I don't like to pry, but…" Nothing could be further from the truth.

Senior-living homes are notorious haunts of busybodies. Said one ninety-six year old of the *much* older ninety-eight year old who lived next door, "I've never met a woman who was as much of a busybody as that man. Never!"

And as Jen Chaney says of Gladys Denker, a character in *Downton Abbey*, " She drinks too much, she's a busybody, she brags, she blackmails and she's just super-annoying."[22]

---

[22]Jen Chaney, "The 20 Most Despicable Characters in Downton Abbey History" (<*https://www.vulture.com/2016/02/downton-abbey-most-despicable-characters-ever.html*>)

Crumbs

Obviously, the word "crumbs" itself doesn't come from the English Bible any more than the "bread" they might have come from. "Crumbs" is shorthand here for a number of forms of an idiom that *does* come from the Bible: "I (you, he, they, etc.) get the crumbs;" "I'm left with the crumbs:" "they give us the crumbs." Etc.

Matthew 15:27 "Truth, Lord: yet the dogs eat of the crumbs which fall from their masters' table."

A Canaanite woman had asked Jesus to help her daughter. Jesus observed to her that his mission was to Israelites. She was insistent, and he answered again that one doesn't take children's bread and toss it to the family dogs. The woman was not to be outdone. She responded with the remark about crumbs, and thus was born the idiom.

The idiom, which might be "the crumbs that fall from the master's table," is commonly reduced to its core word, "crumbs." Once simplified, it's then recombined with anything else the writer or speaker may be talking about. Examples abound of the crumbs coming from bread, cake, cookies, a sandwich, meat, or anything else. Metaphors are sometimes mixed. But usually it's just that somebody *got* "the crumbs."

A former girlfriend spilled more than we really should know about her on a love-advice blog: "I'm really hurt by how he is treating his new girlfriend. It's seems like she is getting the best of him. While I got the crumbs."[23]

A Yankee fan was bitter over being last when he's so devoted to the team: "The problem with this stadium is that they put all the money into the areas that the rich, the players,

---

[23] http://www.dearcupid.org/question/my-ex-treats-his-present-girlfriend-so-much .html

and the press will see and enjoy. Not the average fan. We got the crumbs."[24]

An environmentalist envies the treatment of high profile organizations: "The big green groups can get any amount of money that they request, but the groups that are on the ground—the ones that are down in the trenches—we get the crumbs off the table."[25]

In 2018 then Vice President Mike Pence responded to a Democrat who likened the recently passed tax cuts to "crumbs." Pence said, "Any leader in America that would say $1,000 in the pockets of working families is crumbs is out of touch with the American people."

A small business owner said of her strategy: "Most of my business is through dealers and midsize and large organizations. We get the crumbs off the table, which is enough."[26]

This last lady understood the original sense of the Canaanite woman's wry logic. The Canaanite understood that Jesus was sparring with her, testing her. She didn't take offense at his remark about dogs—none had been meant. She understood that a Jewish prophet would be sent by his God to the Jewish people. She just presented to Jesus the principle that God's blessing on the Jews would trickle down to the Gentiles. In this case, fall from the table. She intended to take advantage of the crumbs.

---

[24](https://bats.blogs.nytimes.com/2009/04/03/challenge-of-the-new-yankee-stadium)
[25](https://www.insidephilanthropy.com/home/2017/12/12/report-foundations-are-underfunding-climate-vulnerable-communities-in-the-south)
[26] (https://www.inc.com/magazine/201509/deirdre-van-dyk/2015-inc5000-the-best-way-to-launch-a-business.html)

Can a leopard change his spots?

With a nod to Rudyard Kipling's tale of *How the Leopard Got His Spots,* we know that try as he might (and he doesn't) the leopard cannot erase his spots—(technically, "rosettes"). The truism presented itself to the prophet Jeremiah as a natural illustration of a spiritual principle:

Jeremiah 13:23 "Can the Ethiopian change his skin, or the leopard his spots? then may ye also do good, that are accustomed to do evil."

Jeremiah's prophecy was that the judgment of God was inevitable because Israel could no more stop sinning than a person can change his skin color or an animal his markings. If they could have, then God would have relented.

Did Jeremiah believe people's essential nature is immutable, or was he engaging in hyperbole? It's fair to say that prophecy is often laced with hyperbole, as is a great deal of the rest of the Bible: "And there went out unto him all the land of Judaea, and they of Jerusalem" (Mark 1:5) is an example. "He came unto his own, and his own received him not" is another, as witnessed by the very next phrase: "But as many as received him…" The point of Jeremiah's remark is that Israel was bent on self destruction because their sin was profoundly ingrained.

It's similar to saying you can't teach an old dog new tricks (*not* in the Bible, by the way). Well, you can, but it isn't at all easy.

A little research turns up the claim that the leopard-spot idiom comes from a Greek proverb. Perhaps, but it isn't easy to find anywhere. It may have existed in some obscure Greek writings, but the Hebrew scriptures popularized it. The English language got its saying from old Jeremiah. In English, the saying first appeared in 1546.

Casting the first stone

Wictionary gives a good everyday definition for this phrase: "To act self-righteously in accusing another person, believing oneself to be blameless." Wictionary illustrates from a statement by Newt Gingrich in 2007 in *The Guardian*, that he had hesitated to vote for the impeachment of President Clinton. "I knew I couldn't cast the first stone as I knew I had weaknesses."[27]

Gingrich, of course, as a Christian, knew where "casting the first stone" comes from:

John 8:7 "So when they continued asking him, he lifted up himself, and said unto them, He that is without sin among you, let him first cast a stone at her."

The original statement was a masterful answer to a tricky question, a setup contrived by devious legalists to trip up Jesus. The question was what Jesus said should be done to a woman caught committing adultery and dragged into Jesus' presence (without the offending man, by the way). Moses said stone her. What did Jesus say, the scribes and Pharisees asked?

Jesus' answer did *not* deny the authority that had been given to Moses to establish the law. It merely directed the scribes and Pharisees to line up to do the stoning on the basis of their relative innocence. Jesus was preaching an entirely different sermon, one not about what was just punishment, but rather whether anyone was without sin.

Unfortunately, the misuse of "casting the first stone" is common. Ben Giselbach points out that many people quote it in an attempt to defend themselves against Christian witness or preaching. Says Giselbach, "When we divorce Jesus' statement from its immediate context in an effort to undermine

---

[27] (https://www.theguardian.com/world/2007/mar/10/usa.edpilkington)

a legitimate condemnation of sin, we are just as guilty as the scribes and Pharisees who were abusing the Law themselves."[28]

Oh, and the phrase is not only commonly misused, but it's also commonly misquoted as "Let he who is without sin cast the first stone" (as in *The Independent, The Telegraph* and *The Irish Times* (UK), and even *The Free Dictionary)*. It's amazing how many people, confronted with Elizabethan English, not only insert thee's and thou's where they don't belong and add "-eth" and "-est" to verbs when they don't need them, but they also let grammar go out the window. It's "*He* who is without sin" (NASB, KJV, etc.) but "Let *him* who is without sin" (NIV, ESV, etc.).

Star Trek: Deep Space Nine erroneously titled an episode with the "Let he who is without sin" ungrammatical misquotation. And a blog called WWUTT operated by First Southern Baptist Church in Junction City, Kansas, uses the misquoted and ungrammatical phrase as a title to an article, right above a picture that shows someone with a sign clearly quoting the verse *correctly*. Go figure. Interestingly, WWUTT (When We Understand The Text) concludes that article by saying of the Johannine text about the adulterous woman, "It's a nice story, but it has no original authorship, and doesn't belong in the Bible." Oh, really?

I understand the issues with John 7:53-8:11. However, there's no doubt that the church in A.D. 325 put its stamp of approval on the gospel of John as it was, including the story of the woman taken in adultery. It's in the Bible, and in my book, there it stays.

---

[28]Ben Giselbach, "He Who is Without Sin, Cast the First Taken-Out-Of-Context Stone," https://plainsimplefaith.com/he-who-is-without-sin-cast-the-first-taken-out-of-context-stone , May 14, 2014, The Internet; Accessed 12/20/2018).

Casting your pearls before swine

Besides being a cartoon strip by Stephan Pastis, the name of a rock band, and multiple song and album titles, "pearls before swine" is an expression first spoken by Jesus:

Matthew 7:6 "Give not that which is holy unto the dogs, neither cast ye your pearls before swine, lest they trample them under their feet, and turn again and rend you."

The context of the verse doesn't help us much in figuring out what Jesus meant. It sits amidst other pithy sayings in the Sermon on the Mount. Immediately preceding it is a verse about hypocrisy, and right after it is a saying about seeking God for answers and blessings. There has never been much controversy, however, about what casting pearls before swine means. Christ meant that his followers should not spend inordinate amounts of time trying to present and explain the gospel and other Bible teachings to people who have no interest or who, even worse, who are inclined to twist it and respond by attacking.

More generally, the secular culture has adopted the phrase (though with infrequent usage) to mean "wasting ...time by offering something that is helpful or valuable to someone who does not appreciate or understand it."[29]

Examples of the repetition of this proverb in modern life include not only Christians talking about not wasting their resources on lost causes, but also anti-Christians (or at least anti-conservative-Christians) weighing in on the far distant, other side. Frank Schaeffer counseled President Obama, "As you showed us again at your press conference of Feb 9, you are a brilliant, articulate and decent man. Your Republican

---

[29]Collins English Dictionary

opponents are not decent people but ideologues bent on destroying you. To quote the biblical adage sir, don't cast your pearls before swine."[30] Persons unfamiliar with Schaeffer should know that he burned out in fundamentalist Christian circles and became an enemy of fundamentalism, religious and political conservatism, and all Republicans—if that wasn't already obvious.

Clearly, the speaker's social, religious, moral, or political point of view determines what he thinks are pearls and whom he considers to be swine.

The phrase has invited deliberate but wry misusage. In 1938 the *Spectator* published this social note:

It is recorded that Mrs. Parker and a snooty debutante were both going in to supper at a party: the debutante made elaborate way, saying sweetly "Age before beauty, Mrs. Parker." "And pearls before swine," said Mrs. Parker, sweeping in.[31]

The retort was later credited to Claire Boothe Luce.

---

[30]Frank Schaeffer, "An Open Letter to President Obama" (Huffington Post, 5/25/2011)
[31]*The Spectator* (London, Sept 16, 1938).

Charity begins at home

The first use we can find of the phrase "Charity begins at home" in print was in Thomas Browne's 1642 book *Religio Medici*: "Charity begins at home, is the voice of the World..." Browne used the phrase implying it was a saying that predated his writing. English playwright John Marston wrote a play (or perhaps only revised one), *Histrio Mastix*, published in 1610 containing the line, "True charity beginneth first at home." John Wyclif had expressed the same idea as early as 1382, in *Of Prelates*: "Charite schuld bigyne at hem-self."

The logic and sentiment of the phrase may ultimately be based on two Bible passages, one from the pen of Paul the Apostle: **"But if any provide not for his own, and specially for those of his own house, he hath denied the faith, and is worse than an infidel" (1 Timothy 5:8)**. The other would be Leviticus 19:18: "Love thy neighbor as thyself: I am the Lord."

We'll concede that the form most often found in English is best attributed to Marston and Browne. We should also point out that interpreting the proverb requires understanding that in the earliest English Bibles, the word "charity" could be rendered simply "love."

The meaning of the saying or proverb varies with the speaker. It has been notably used as a defense for taking care of one's own needs before expending money and energy on others. Consequently it has been used to oppose a nation's foreign aid and to explain why pleas from charitable organizations are turned down. This usage probably traces to an interpretation of "love thy neighbor as thyself" that focuses on the fact that to love someone else you must first have a fundamental love of yourself, which we usually call a healthy self respect. The irony is that the speaker sometimes lauds charity to rationalize stinginess.

This was the sense given the proverb by Marston, whose character Pry (Pride) said:

True charity beginneth first at home,
Heere in your bosomes dwell your deere-lov'd hearts,
Feed them with ioy; first crowne their appetites,
And then cast water on the care-scorch't face,
Let your owne longings first be satisfied,
All other pitty is but foolish pryde.

Before using the proverb as Marston did, it's wise to note who said it in his play.

Browne's use of the proverb was not far from Marston's. Browne contrasted the common use of the saying with people's self destructive tendencies:

But how shall we expect charity towards others, when we are uncharitable to ourselves? "Charity begins at home," is the voice of the world; yet is every man his greatest enemy, and as it were his own executioner.

Browne further criticized the sense of the proverb as it was used in his day. He alleged that people retreated from outgoing love by keeping their affections within their homes:

That a man should lay down his life for his friend seems strange to vulgar affections and such as confine themselves within that worldly principle, "Charity begins at home."

The proverb, it seems, is best employed to explain how people develop a propensity to loving others in the first place, and to exhort them to do it: learn at home to love one another, and to be kind and generous. Then go out and love others, too.

Cross to bear

This phrase categorically comes from the Bible:

Luke 14:27 "And whosoever doth not bear his cross, and come after me, cannot be my disciple."

Jesus contemplated his soon-coming experience of dying on a Roman cross; he characterized the life every follower of his should live as an imitation of him; and then told any would-be disciple that the cross was mandatory. The cross was the exemplar, the essence, of the Christian's self denial and acceptance of the absolute Lordship of Jesus, no matter what.

It's an extraordinary shame that "one's cross to bear" has descended to meaning little more than "a burden or trial one must put up with."[32] Many people who have little connection to Christianity or churches can be found using the phrase, however, and this superficial meaning is the one they give it.

A great many songs, books, television program episodes and other endeavors have included "cross to bear" in their titles, when the themes of the works had little or nothing to do with Christianity or Christ. The leading online dictionaries of the day include listings of "cross to bear" with definitions that don't even refer to Jesus (Merriam-Webster, Cambridge Dictionary, etc.). A certain doctor says that diagnosing and telling his patients they have cancer is his cross to bear.[33]

Adding the article "a" to the idiom is an indication of its diminished meaning. "*A* cross to bear" is worlds apart from "bear his cross." The cross, in the source of the idiom, is not one of several things one must bear: it encompasses the whole burden, the discipline, the responsibility, of the life one accepts if he becomes a follower of Jesus.

---

[32] Dictionary.com
[33] The Millennial Doctor, *https://reflectionsofamillennialdoctor.com/*.

Nowhere in the Bible after Jesus said what he did about the cross and then hung on the cross on Calvary does any New Testament author ever itemize crosses or treat the concept as generally describing problems or hardships. That's a much later development.

Yet these days we learn that Gregg Allman wants us to think that his hard experience with drugs, failed romances and life as a rock star was his cross to bear. The president of the Farmers' Union wants us regard climate change as our cross to bear. A writer looking at the Jubilee Anniversary of *Brown v. Board of Education* says that lingering racial inequality in educational performance is blacks' cross to bear.[34] A Maryland Terrapins player who's had a hard time getting signed to pro ball wants us to think it's just his cross to bear. And, at the other end of the spectrum, one songwriter and guitarist says to his girlfriend that "Love is Our Cross to Bear."[35]

Finally, Millennials, those persons reaching young adulthood in the early 21st century, have been characterized as "the generation that can't get off their phones and the generation that doesn't know how to interact with other people." But that's not their fault: they've been inundated by technology invented by their parents, and the 'burden' of that technology is "The Millennial's Cross to Bear."[36]

Sorry. Not a cross. But that's today's English for you.

---

[34]James D. Anderson, "Crosses to Bear and Promises to Keep: The Jubilee Anniversary of Brown v. Board of Education" (*https://journals.sagepub.com/doi/10.1177/0042085904265150*).

[35]John Gorka (*https://www.20summers.org/events/videos/2018/10/25/john-gorka-select-songs-nazarene-guitar-love-is-our-cross-to-bear-when-the-doves-cry-prince*).

[36]Jordan Bohannon, "Technology: The Millennial's Cross to Bear" (*The State Press*, 4/28/14) Available from: *http://www.statepress.com/article/2014/04/technology-the-millennials-cross-to-bear*, The Internet; Accessed 12/21/18.

Death, where is thy sting

This phrase might have gone into the list at the end of this book as one that is almost never used outside the churchgoing community, except for the contention argued here that the word "sting" and particularly the phrase "take the sting out" preserve the Pauline construction.

Hosea 13:14 "Death, where are your barbs? Sheol, where is your sting?" (HCSV)

1 Corinthians 15:55 "O death, where is thy sting? O grave, where is thy victory?"

The Old Testament contains ten or more references to a "sting," more than half of which are used figuratively to refer to the effects of insults, alcohol, or punishment in general. When Paul wrote his famous line about the sting of death having been removed by the sacrifice of Christ that saves us from the *second* death, he was loosely quoting the prophet Hosea. The King James doesn't render Hosea's Hebrew word *debareka* as "sting," but rather "plagues," as does the ISV. NASB has "thorns," which do sting, as the author can attest. CSB similarly has "barbs," as does Holman, quoted above, but Holman translates the word in the next phrase "sting" (which KJV renders as "destruction"). A survey of a dozen more translations reveals that most like "plagues." But Paul apparently liked "sting" in the first part and "victory" in the latter. Who are we to argue?

The single word "sting" used figuratively probably derives from the biblical use, but there's little doubt that the phrase "take the sting out" does come from the Bible. This is the sense Hosea and Paul gave it: the removal of the pain of something unavoidable.

Clothier reporter Suzy Menkes wrote: "Blame it on the

bankers and the hedge fund executives—not to mention the politicians—who have people using the word "suits" with spitting contempt. For the overriding theme of the Paris menswear season, which opened Thursday, is to promote smart casual looks and take the sting out of suits."[37] We're not sure why suits became an enemy uniform, but it happened somewhere in the author's lifetime.

Cook County Commissioner Richard Boykin commenting on his ruminations on possible cannabis laws says: "We keep on incarcerating people...I think we have got to look at legalizing marijuana to take the sting out of it."[38] A little pot probably takes the sting out of whatever else is going on,[39] but it comes back when the high is gone.

---

[37]Suzy Menkes, "Taking the Sting Out of Suits," https://www.nytimes.com/2010/06/25/fashion/25iht-rblame.html, The Internet, Accessed 2 Jan 2019
[38]http://chronicleillinois.com/news/cook-county-news/cook-commissioner-legalizing-pot-take-sting/
[39]So the author is informed. Though a child of the 60s, he never tried marijuana, or alcoholic beverages in any form.

Den of thieves

Besides being the title of a 2018 film and a 2012 novel, "den of thieves" is an idiom meaning a place frequented or inhabited by thieves, whether literal or figurative.

Matthew 21:13 "It is written, My house shall be called the house of prayer; but ye have made it a den of thieves."

Jesus' accusation was leveled at everyone involved, explicitly or implicitly, in the practice of buying and selling animals for sacrifice in the outer court of the temple in Jerusalem. Of the profane things that Jews might have done, this was high on the list of seriousness. Not only was it a desecration of the holy place, but because the sellers had the buyers over a barrel, they routinely gouged them—thus, they were thieves as well as purveyors of sacrilege.

The phrase today has liberal use in print media, being a popular accusation against any business or organization perceived to be cheating people (including the IRS).

Michael Harris, the CEO of River Wealth Management, says that after being out of money management for a while, he returned to investing in the stock market, although "I thought it was a den of thieves and crooks and a lot of unsavory folks." This author held that opinion earlier in life, until he realized his retirement fund was largely in the stock market, and then he eagerly checked regularly to see how his thieves were doing.

President Donald Trump fired FBI director James Comey in 2017 over various issues as well as the recommendations of the Attorney General and the Deputy AG. Trump later said, "I did a great service to the people in firing him...I think Comey was the ringleader in this whole den of thieves."

A Texas man whom Bank of America charged six dollars to cash his payroll check complained about the policy and said that "the policy sucks and Bank of America is nothing but a den of thieves!! They don't care about anything but making a dishonest dollar!!"[40]

In an interesting twist on the usual accusations, Pastor James David Manning of Atlah Worldwide Church, webcasted a fiery denouncement of an LGBT congregation that wanted to buy his church facilities. A state judge had ordered the facilities sold to pay taxes and other debts. Manning spewed obscenities at the LGBT fellowship and told them essentially that until gay men could give birth (we've summarized the actual words he used) they weren't going to get his church. A person leaving a comment on the website found Manning himself reprehensible and said, "The *Church* is nothing but a den of thieves."

[40]William M., https://www.yelp.com/biz/bank-of-america-lubbock-6, The Internet, Accessed 2 Jan 2019.

Don't go to bed angry

Great advice, this, for all couples in particular. In its most modern form, we believe it is based on the scriptural admonition given by Paul:

Ephesians 4:26 "Be ye angry, and sin not: let not the sun go down upon your wrath."

More modern versions clarify that the Greek doesn't command us to get angry; its sense is, if or when we get angry, which we all do, don't get carried away. The second part of this admonition instructs us to repair things quickly, if possible before the day ends. Brooding, rehearsing our irritations, allowing anger to fester, can produce nothing good.

In view of the source of this advice (which gave it as much more than advice, by the way), it's surprising how many people in the business of counseling these days pooh pooh the biblical instruction.

Says Amie M. Gordon, ("Ph.D", she reminds us) of Psychology Today: "'Never go to bed angry' might be one of the worst pieces of old-time wisdom. People tend to feel more negative emotions and react more strongly to negative events when they are tired. So finding yourself fighting late at night—when you should be sleeping—is a recipe for disaster." Notice that Gordon assumes that anger leads to quarrels (which it doesn't always) and that quarrels take place late at night (which they probably don't any more than at any other time of day). Gordon seems fixated (to fire back one her psychological terms at her) on the inevitability of habitual, heated fighting in marriages or relationships, which suggests that she is projecting her clinical experience upon the entire population.

Scott Christian, who writes on relationships, opines that not going to bed angry is "great advice provided you (a) don't actually need sleep, and (b) become increasingly rational as exhaustion overtakes you. But for the rest of us, the 95 percent of us who make far better decisions when fully rested, this age-old chestnut is probably something to avoid."[41] We think Mr. Christian isn't aware that the "chestnut" comes from the Bible. At any rate, his assumption that the proverb (which we could call it) means couples should stay up til all hours arguing, misses the point.

But that's what Jim Daly, of Focus on the Family, thinks it means. Said Daly in his blog on June 4, 2018, "Don't go to bed angry: stay up and fight!" Admittedly, Daly was playing with us a little bit. He gave the reader guidelines for fair fighting, including never doing it in front of children, never becoming physical, and never throwing around the word "divorce."

One senior citizen interviewed about having lived by the proverb said, "You never go to bed angry because you don't know if you'll have that person in the morning."[42]

That actually happened to Ashley Murrell whose husband Mikey came home late from one of his frequent sixteen-hour shifts. She was angry and complained about it, and they fought. Mikey had only been trying to work extra to make life better for them both. He went to bed on the sofa. In the morning Ashley found him just as he had collapsed there. He was grey and cold, quite dead. When she was able later to offer her perspective she said, "Life is too short to go to bed angry."[43]

[41]https://www.thenest.com/content/dont-believe-what-they-say-go-to-bed-angry
[42]https://www.huffingtonpost.com/karl-a-pillemer-phd/marriage-advice_b_3740376.html
[43]Carolina Picard, "Don't go to bed angry, widow warns" https://www.goodhousekeeping.com/life/relationships/news/a45047/ashley-murrell-husband-sofa/

Don't let your left hand know what your right hand is doing

This idiomatic expression appears in various closely related forms, sometimes the simple statement that the left hand doesn't know, etc. Occasionally the right hand gets first mention, but the original form is this:

Matthew 6:3 "But when thou doest alms, let not thy left hand know what thy right hand doeth."

The point of his teaching was that Christian giving was to be discrete, not announced for public knowledge. Jesus may have called upon an existing Aramaism for his saying. But because he said it, we have it.

A good magician can make it seem that there is little to nothing going on between his hands, when there very well is. But the whole point of his surreptitious slight of hand is to convince his audience that he's not up to anything. What Jesus meant by his saying about giving was similar: people looking at us should not see charity for display. His saying was less about the effect of giving than the motive. As he said just before in Matthew 6:1, "Be careful not to do your acts of righteousness before men, *to be seen by them*" (emphasis ours).

Jesus didn't mean that absolutely no one should know about that check in the offering plate, or the gift to the free medical clinic. In fact, charities other than churches often have named giving levels where donors are listed (unless they specifically request not to be). The function of these named groups is both to acknowledge the supporters and to inspire others to give. The publication of the levels and their members is generally not made to anyone but other supporters, anyway. Lower level givers, however, sometimes say they were motivated to increase giving because they saw how others had put their money where their hearts were.

Art Carden, an Assistant Economics professor at Rhodes

College, says very public giving—such as in government give-away programs—tends to "worsen the problems people are trying to solve, because they change incentives." He concludes that "if you just want to give people stuff, though, then your charity is most effective when it is given in secret."[44]

But the left-hand right-hand expression appears in many contexts unrelated to charity.

"In Afghanistan, Uncle Sam's left hand doesn't know what his right hand is doing," wrote Erin Dunne about how the CIA is conducting military strikes while other U.S. forces are trying to establish the rule of law.[45]

Gordon Logan and Matthew Crump have noticed what a lot of us who "touch type" have, which is that if you think too much about what you're typing, you'll start making mistakes. Logan and Crump suggest that in typing, in fact, the left hand really doesn't know what the right hand is doing, or more technically the brain suppresses the individual functions in favor of the synchrony.[46]

Dictionary.com illustrates the meaning of the expression as uncoordinated actions, such as in, "Purchasing has placed the order and accounting says we can't pay for more supplies this month; the left hand doesn't know what the right hand is doing."

---

[44]Art Carden, "Improve your charitable giving" (https://www.lifehack.org/articles/money/improve-your-charitable-giving-let-not-your-left-hand-know-what-your-right-is-doin.html)

[45]Erin Dunne, (https://www.washingtonexaminer.com/opinion/in-afghanistan-uncle-sams-left-hand-doesnt-know-what-his-right-hand-is-doing)

[46]Logan, Gordon D., and Matthew J. C. Crump. "The Left Hand Doesn't Know What the Right Hand Is Doing: The Disruptive Effects of Attention to the Hands in Skilled Typewriting." Psychological Science, vol. 20, no. 10, Oct. 2009, pp. 1296–1300, doi:10.1111/j.1467-9280.2009.02442.x.

Dreamer of dreams

It doesn't appear in everyday conversation, but "dreamer of dreams" catches the imagination of artists, poets, and writers from generation to generation. It comes from the pen of Moses:

Deuteronomy 13:1 "If there arise among you a prophet, or a dreamer of dreams, and giveth thee a sign or a wonder…"

Since earliest times people have claimed to have a word from God imparted through a dream. Some have laid claim to a general gift to dream what is going to come to pass, or what God wants people to do. The Bible records numerous incidents of people's having genuine dream revelation, but it also describes some people who faked it. Moses' warning was about fakers.

Ode, by Arthur O'Shaughnessy, was an 1873 poem that began, "We are the music-makers, / And we are the dreamers of dreams, / Wandering by lone sea-breakers / And sitting by desolate streams." O'Shaughnessy makes numerous biblical references in this short poem about the people in any generation who move cultures and civilizations on to greater things.

S. M. Johnson was a nineteenth century minister and later extensive traveler who championed the building of roads throughout the nation. In his brief biography of Johnson, Richard Weingroff calls him "A Dreamer of Dreams."[47]

The Coral Gables Museum styles its Gables Bike Tour as "Dreamer of Dreams." It's a Father's Day tour celebrating the founder of the city, George Merrick.

---

[47]Richard F. Weingroff, "Dr. S. M. Johnson: A Dreamer of Dreams" (https://www.fhwa .dot.gov/infrastructure/johnson.cfm) The Internet, Accessed 3 Jan 2019.

Drop in a bucket

Who hasn't said this? A company being sued by a customer offers to settle for a thousand dollars, but he replies that the offer is a drop in a bucket: he wants a million.

Merriam-Webster says the expression means "a part so small as to be negligible." That's just the meaning the Hebrew gave it under the pen of the prophet:

Isaiah 40:15 "Behold, the nations are as a drop of a bucket, and are counted as the small dust of the balance: behold, he taketh up the isles as a very little thing."

"Bucket" here is perhaps the entirety of creation. Had the ancients known what we know they might have thought of the bucket as the solar system and the universe as a barrel. At any rate, while human beings vaunt the importance, magnificence or power of this nation, that nation or that empire, to God they are next to nothing. They are a drop in a bucket.

Miles Raymer, a contributor to Pitchfork.com, wrote about will.i.am, an American rap artist, who launched a brand called Ekocycle, that turns plastic bottles into consumer goods, such as bedsheets. The W Hotel chain signed up to have Ekocycle provide the sheets for all forty-six of their hotels, "the equivalent, according to their figures, of diverting 268,000 20 oz. plastic bottles from the waste stream. That's a respectable amount, although with Americans consuming tens of billions of gallons of bottled beverages per year, it's a drop in a bucket the size of Lake Michigan."[48]

---

[48]Miles Raymer, "Consumer goods and bads" (https://pitchfork.com/thepitch/797-consumer-goods-and-bads-laying-on-williams-recycled-plastic-sheets/) Accessed 22 Jan 2019.

Eat drink and be merry

This phrase has not just one but four sources in the Bible:

Isaiah 22:13: "And behold joy and gladness, slaying oxen, and killing sheep, eating flesh, and drinking wine: let us eat and drink; for to morrow we shall die."

In this reference, the context makes clear that the eating and drinking were reveling or resignation to the brevity of life. Isaiah was not recommending a course of enjoyment through fine dining.

Ecclesiastes 8:15: "Then I commended mirth, because a man hath no better thing under the sun, than to eat, and to drink, and to be merry: for that shall abide with him of his labour the days of his life, which God giveth him under the sun."

Solomon framed the thought differently by adding "joyful," in a context that made clear he was recommending that humanity enjoy the world God has given us.

Later, the Apostle Paul contrasted his confidence in facing persecution and even death for the gospel, with the mere resignation of people who think since they're going to die anyway, they might as well live it up while they're here:

1 Corinthians 15:32: "If after the manner of men I have fought with beasts at Ephesus, what advantageth it me, if the dead rise not? let us eat and drink; for to morrow we die."

The final verse comes from one of the gospels and was spoken by Jesus in the Parable of the Rich Fool:

Luke 12:19: "And I will say to my soul, Soul, thou hast much goods laid up for many years; take thine ease, eat, drink, and be merry."

In context, the fool was a rich man who ran out of barns for his wildly successful crops. He built more—apparently not even considering the possibility of giving to the poor what wouldn't fit in the barns he already had—and then he sat back and planned how he was going to enjoy life.

Our "eat, drink, and be merry" is often paired with "for tomorrow you (or we) die," in some conflation of two or more of the verses above. Usually if we say "merry" we don't follow it with any thought of dying. The phrase has a fraternal twin: one is an optimist, the other a pessimist.

Outside of the context of church and synagogue, the average English speaker today who uses some form of "eat, drink and be merry" is recommending celebration.

A gallery in Asheville, NC, advertises a holiday event showcasing holiday dining decor and inviting people to come and "eat, drink and be merry!"

"Eat, Drink and Be Merry" is the name of a catering and party planning service in New York City. No hint is there of any resignation to the certainty of oncoming death.

And some authors brave the nattering nay-bobs of "healthy choices" and actually recommend eating, drinking and being merry to live longer. Says one, "The health conscious, work-out world of the 1990s could in fact be doing more damage to people because of the guilt it instills in those who seek a modicum of physical pleasure through eating, drinking or just lolling about."[49]

---

[49]Steve Connor, "Secret of a long life: eat, drink and be merry" (*The Independent*, October 16, 1995).

Eleventh hour

In this digital age, there are some young people who have to have "clockwise" and "counterclockwise" explained to them. Before the invention of the clock movement, making possible the division of the hour into sixty minutes and the minute into sixty seconds, the transition from previous systems was even more dramatic. Before that, people generally just said it was the fourth hour, etc. In biblical Jewish culture, the day lasted from sunset to sunset. (Thus, "the evening and [then] the morning were the first day" - Genesis 1:5.) One would say that an event began at the sixth hour (equatorial noon) or the ninth hour (in an ideal sense, 3:00 p.m.). Something that happened at the eleventh hour happened just one hour before the end of the day, which would have been around 6:00 p.m.

"The eleventh hour," then, in the Bible anyway, was about 5:00 p.m. The phrase has come down into English mostly in a figurative sense: the final moment when something can be accomplished before its opportunity expires.

Matthew 20:6 "And about the eleventh hour he went out, and found others standing idle, and saith unto them, Why stand ye here all the day idle?"

It's *endekatan* in Greek, meaning simply "the eleventh." The "hour" is understood. In Jesus' telling of the parable of the laborers, the detail about the hours was significant. The owner of the vineyard went out at the third, sixth, ninth, and finally the eleventh hour to hire people to work in his harvest. The idiom, "the eleventh hour," rose quickly in English because of its association with the idea of a last moment opportunity.

In Western time calculation the eleventh hour naturally brings thoughts of an hour before midnight. It hardly matters to the idiomatic use, but keeping in mind the fact that sundown was the end of the Jewish day—the end of effective light, the end of work, the beginning of night and restricted activity—helps us to understand the anticipation of cessation that would have been associated with the last hour in the day.

Tony McDonald warned Texans in late 2014 that there was movement underfoot to gag Texans if they were critical of government, and he called it "Speech Regulation at the Eleventh Hour."[50] We hope Tony has many brethren willing to keep watch over enemies of the First Amendment to the Constitution of the United States.

"Palliative Care at the Eleventh Hour" is a moving piece by Dr. Anirudh Ramesh at Johns Hopkins Hospital. He describes in detail his emotional ordeal in trying to extend the life and then relieve the suffering of a patient dying from kidney failure. The eleventh hour was first that of his patient, but in a profound way, that of Ramesh as well.[51]

And as Pat Burson reminds us frantically: "Tomorrow is Valentine's Day. Did you forget again? Even with all the TV commercials, Lifetime lovey-dovey movie marathons and subtle reminders from your sweetie, you still have arrived at the eleventh hour with nothing planned for the two of you?"[52] Ooo! Thanks for the reminder, Pat. In spite of assurances that Valentine's Day doesn't matter, secretly it probably does. And anyway, absolutely nobody minds a fuss being made over their being loved. Don't let it get to the eleventh hour this year before getting those roses, because if you do, they'll all be picked over.

---

[50]Tony McDonald, "Speech Regulation at the Eleventh Hour" (https://texasscorecard .com/features/speech-regulation-at-the-eleventh-hour/)

[51]Ramesh A (2015) Palliative Care at the Eleventh Hour. J Palliat Care Med 5: e135.

[52]Pat Burson, "Loving Suggestions for Lovers" (https://www.newsday.com/ entertainment/music/valentine-s-day-loving-suggestions-for-lovers-1.893543)

Ends of the earth

Depending on the version you search, "ends of the earth" appears as many as twenty-eight times in the Bible and is widely agreed to originate in the Hebrew language of the Old Testament. The King James contains more than a dozen instances of the phrase, the oldest of which is in Job:

Job 37:3 "He directeth it under the whole heaven, and his lightning unto the ends of the earth."

It's not an especially creative phrase. It take no great feat of imagination to come up with it, especially in an ancient world where often the cosmology had it that the earth was flat—perhaps round, but not spherical—and that it had both corners and ends, or edges. It's worth arguing that various places in the Bible where expressions such as "ends of the earth," "the four winds," and so on, are used, the authors are speaking metaphorically, even as we do today. We even mix our metaphors. Whoever heard of a globe having four corners? Yet we say it. It's hypocrisy to accuse the Bible of actually teaching that the earth is flat; its authors merely used the imagery of the day, just as we still do.

But back to the phrase. It simply means, "as far as you can go." And it can be a good thing, or not:

"I'll hunt you down to the ends of the earth!"

"I'll go to the ends of the earth to please you."

Evil eye

This idiom occurs in the King James Bible three times.

Proverbs 28:22 "He that hasteth to be rich hath an evil eye, and considereth not that poverty shall come upon him."

The Hebrew behind the term "evil eye" means just that, whereas in Proverbs 23:6 the Hebrew is different, but the KJV still renders it "evil eye." The Greek also has "evil eye" in Mark 7:22. In both the Old and New Testaments having an evil eye was the term for being a miser, or being stingy. It isn't hard to figure out how people came up with the term. There's just this look, sometimes, isn't there?!

Interestingly, however, the term doesn't very often mean "stingy" these days. It's usually found in the expression "to give someone the evil eye." This usage probably borrows heavily from other cultures in which it was believed (and perhaps still is in some places) that a person with bewitching or magical powers can transmit a curse by casting his eye on someone, especially if the target stares back.

Merchants are making a killing off evil-eye items these days. An Amazon.com search of "evil eye" yields more than 10,000 results, mostly in the form of jewelry.

It isn't always spoken with deadly seriousness. ReShonda Billingsley writes in her novel, *A Good Man Is Hard to Find*, that Ava "noticed Cliff watching her sister's backside with a grin on his face. Cliff caught himself and turned his attention back to Ava...'What did I do? She's cute.' Ava gave him the evil eye." Okay, maybe it *is* deadly serious after all.[53]

---

[53]ReShonda Tate Billingsley, *A Good Man Is Hard to Find* (New York, Simon and Schuster, 2011) 45..

Exodus

Genesis, Exodus, Leviticus, Numbers, Deuteronomy

The English word by itself comes from both the Greek *(exodou)* and Latin *(exodos)*, by way of the Bible, where the Greek of the Septuagint (a Greek translation of the Hebrew Old Testament) says in the second book of the Pentateuch that the children of Israel "went out" of the land of Egypt. The word was seized upon for the title of the book, by Moses: "Exodus."

It later came to refer as well to Israel's leaving Babylon. Much, much later "Exodus" was the title of a 1960 film by Otto Preminger, the story of the modern day founding of the nation Israel in 1948.

However, the word needn't be, and it isn't, restricted to such lofty subjects. Some of us say we're going to make an early exodus when leaving a party that has become too rowdy or that is about to become so.

A pastor took his exodus to a teaching position at a nearby college, prompting his congregation's profession of profuse tears.

One elderly North Carolina lady "eagerly and anxiously took her exodus from her earthly tabernacle," said her obituary, when she died at the modestly ripe age of eighty.

Time magazine wryly writes that "A fortnight ago Correspondent Don Burke closed TIME Inc.'s Cairo bureau and made his exodus from Egypt."[54]

And "Exodus Travels" is a UK firm specializing in, you guessed it, going out from wherever you are, getting away from it all—*leaving!*

---

[54]*Time* (New York, 9/13/1948). Reprinted. at *http://content.time.com/time/magazine/article/0,9171,888449,00.html.*

Eye to eye

This simple phrase means that two or more parties have a common understanding or perspective, that they agree. It's interesting that it comes from a Bible passage where it may not mean what it does today.

Isaiah 52:8: "Thy watchmen shall lift up the voice; with the voice together shall they sing: for they shall see eye to eye, when the LORD shall bring again Zion."

The Hebrew translates "eye to eye," but the key question for translators is what the expression meant when it was written. The answer to that question isn't always obvious.

When the Hebrew scriptures were translated into Greek somewhere in the 3rd century B.C., the scholars had the same challenge. They elected to preserve the same, word-for-word translation: *ophthalmoi pros ophthalmous* —even an ophthalmologist can see what that says. But what does it mean?

A number of translations agree with the King James scholars that the words should be rendered just as they are in the original Hebrew and the meaning derived from the context: "For they shall see eye to eye" (ASV); "for they shall see with eye to eye" (WB); etc. But some highly respected modern translations draw from the context a slightly different meaning of the original Hebrew expression: "For they will see with their own eyes" (NAS); "When the LORD returns to Zion, they will see it with their own eyes" (NIV); "for every eye will see when the LORD returns to Zion" (HCSB); and even, "for before their very eyes they see the Lord returning to Jerusalem" (NLT).

The point is that older, word-for-word translations stick with literal renderings, while some newer translations try to interpret what the Hebrew construction meant to its original hearers. Oddly enough, none appears to take the construction "eye to eye" to mean "agree." The King James doesn't really seem to mean "agree," though one can make approximate sense of the verse with that definition.

There's no question about the meaning today, however. The media, for instance, love to make much of the inter-familial failure of the presidential Bushes to agree:

"During Bush's presidency, then-Senator [Joe] Biden chaired the Foreign Relations Committee, and said he and Bush did not always see eye-to-eye."[55] No surprise there.

"Bush and Cheney didn't always see eye to eye. He revealed that Cheney became 'angry' in 2007 when the president decided not to pardon former Cheney aide I. Lewis 'Scooter' Libby after Libby was sentenced to 30 months in federal prison."[56] Well, you can't pardon everybody.

"Former President George W. Bush and his mother, former First Lady Barbara Bush, apparently don't see eye-to-eye over whether Jeb Bush should run for the White House in 2016."[57] Well, it's moot, now. He did and he didn't make the cut.

Paul Carrack of Mike and the Mechanics sang it memorably in his 1989 hit song, "The Living Years:" "Say it loud, say it clear / You can listen as well as you hear / It's too late when we die / To admit we don't see eye to eye."[58] And many people's eyes fill with tears when they hear that refrain. It hits too close to home.

---

[55]Peter Crimmins, "George W. And Laura Bush honored for their work with returning veterans (WHYY, 9/11/18) Available from *https://whyy.org/articles/george-w-and-laura-bush-honored-for-their-work-with-returning-veterans/*, The Internet.

[56]Today, (11/10/2010) *https://www.today.com/popculture/bush-admits-mistakes-defends-decisions-wbna39976132*, The Internet.

[57]Paul Steinhauser and Ashley Killough, "Should Jeb Run?" (CNN, 11/20/2013) Available at: *http://politicalticker.blogs.cnn.com/category/barbara-bush/page/2/*, The Internet.

[58]"The Living Years," lyrics by B. A. (Brian) Robertson.

Eye for eye, tooth for tooth

The Code of Hammurabi, written sometime during his Mesopotamian reign from 1792 to 1750 B.C., included 282 laws, a number of which enshrine the principle of punishment befitting the crime—at least in Hammurabi's opinion. Examples: "If a son strike his father, his hands shall be hewn off." And, "If a man knock out the teeth of his equal, his teeth shall be knocked out." From such laws many scholars conclude that "an eye for an eye," etc. was paraphrased or summarized.

Perhaps. However, the Code of Hammurabi was lost to history until discovered in 1901 during excavations of Susa in Iran. What *didn't* disappear, however, was the ancient text that memorialized the exact words we know today as the English expression, and that text is the Bible.

Deuteronomy 19:21 "And thine eye shall not pity; but life shall go for life, eye for eye, tooth for tooth, hand for hand, foot for foot."

Out of context, the phrase in Deuteronomy[59] sounds cold and purely retributive. However, the section that ends with this verse lays stress on a fair trial, serious sanctions for false accusers, and punishment that fits the crime, *and nothing further.* For Mosaic law to prescribe an eye for an eye, etc., was a *limitation* of sinful inclinations, a *restriction* on retaliation. But it also codified the high expectation of a just God.

What happened with this and many other Jewish laws was that they were taken out of their legal context, applied perversely in interpersonal matters, and used to justify behavior that made a mockery of God's justice.

Accordingly, when Jesus came on the scene, he put the eye-for-eye law in perspective and then taught how the citizens of

---

[59]The words appear several other places including Exodus 21:24 and Leviticus 24:19.

the kingdom of God were to surpass the conduct of the law-keepers of the Mosaic Covenant. In so doing, he critiqued not the Jewish system of criminal justice but individual, self-righteous conduct:

Matthew 5:38-39 "Ye have heard that it hath been said, An eye for an eye, and a tooth for a tooth. But I say unto you, That ye resist not evil: but whosoever shall smite thee on thy right cheek, turn to him the other also."

In today's world, unfortunately, an eye for an eye usually means what it meant *before* Jesus said what he said:

Author Thane Rosenbaum thinks it's a valuable principle we ought to go by in government: "To me, there's a greater moral outrage in not taking an eye for an eye, or in taking less than an eye for an eye. It's the moral outrage that comes when people feel they can get away with something."[60]

An Eye for an Eye is a book by John Sack documenting the effort by some Jews following World War 2 to exact revenge on Germans for Nazi atrocities. This author has read the book. Knowing what happened between 1939 and 1945, one is mightily tempted to turn a blind eye.

But using "an eye for an eye" as a philosophy of personal justice has—as Jesus implied—disastrous consequences. As is usually attributed to Mohandas Ghandi, "An eye for an eye leaves the whole world blind."

---

[60]Thane Rosenbaum, in an article from an interview with Amy Crawford, "Where An Eye for an Eye Should be the Letter of the Law" (Available from *https://www.smithsonianmag .com/innovation/where-an-eye-for-an-eye-should-be-the-letter-of-the-law-17327997/*, The Internet).

Face of the earth

Often found in the expression "to disappear from the face of the earth," this idiom has also been the title of publications and works of art. It comes from the first Bible book.

Gen.6:7 "I will destroy man whom I have created from the face of the earth."

It shows up again in Genesis 7:4, Exodus 32:12, 33:16, and Psalm 104:30. It always has a fairly literal meaning.

That literal meaning is present, along with a sense of sad mystery, in a piece by Catherine Harnett, who wrote about her pained memories of her father: "William, a helicopter gunner everyone called Wait because he was always late to the tarmac, his flight suit still unzipped, shouting Wait. Wait for me. Who disappeared off the face of the earth."[61]

An ominous tone is struck with the idiom in remarks made by Prime Minister Binyamin Netanyahu, to cadets about to enter the Israeli Army: "The greatest threat from Iran is the threat of nuclear weapons in the hands of a superpower that declares that we should be destroyed from the face of the earth." Amen to that (See: Amen to that).

On the lighter, facetious side, sports writer Ethan Lee said in early 2019, waxing philosophical about the Mississippi State Bulldogs' disappointing season, "Even though MSU underachieved this season, it's not like the world is ending or that the Bulldogs are going to fall off the face of the earth." I feel that way about most sports teams, and frankly about most sports. And if they *did* fall off the face of the earth, I wouldn't be likely to notice.

---

[61]Catherine Harnett, "Off the Face of the Earth" (https://hudsonreview.com/2018/07/ off-the-face-of-the-earth/#.XC5lMM17m00, The Internet, Accessed 3 Jan 2019).

Fainthearted

Deut.20:8 "And the officers shall speak further unto the people, and they shall say, What man is there that is fearful and fainthearted? let him go and return unto his house, lest his brethren's heart faint as well as his heart."

Moses wanted brave soldiers. If a man was coward enough to admit it openly, Moses wanted him to go home. The term crops up again in Isaiah 7:4 where the prophet told Judah's military leaders not to be fainthearted in the presence of Rezin and Pekah.

Tamlin Wightman wrote in 2014 about a couple by the name of Claassen who went on a safari in South Africa. "To get as close as possible to the creatures big and small, the Claassens embarked on a walking safari, which Eric says, 'is really the way to experience wildlife' (not for the fainthearted)."[62] I wholeheartedly agree. I've *seen* videos of lions attacking people. Not a pretty sight.

When her lover died in a kayaking accident, Juliana Buhring got on a bicycle in Naples and rode 18,000 miles through 19 countries. Christian House wrote about it in "How to REALLY cure heartbreak (Clue: Not for the fainthearted)."[63] As someone who has ridden some 22,000 miles through at least 24 of the United States, I can relate. I did it on a small motorcycle cruiser. That, too, is not for the faint of heart.

Seeking Alpha, a website devoted to investing news and tips, describes investing in Bitcoin as "not for the fainthearted." This writer doesn't even exactly understand Bitcoin, much less have the inclination to invest actual money in it.

---

[62] Tamlin Wightman, "My Trip: A Walking Safari is Not for the Fainthearted" (https://www.rhinoafrica.com/en/destinations/kruger-national-park/2962) 3 Jan 2019.
[63] https://www.telegraph.co.uk/women/life/how-to-really-cure-heartbreak-clue-not-for-the-fainthearted/), 3 Jan 2019.

Give me *gold* coins. Now *there's* something for the heart!

And finally, aging is not for the fainthearted. So say many, many experts on health and geriatrics. (There's just something about that word, "geriatrics," that makes this author cringe, here in his 69th year.)

"The key to aging is acceptance; believe me, it is not for the fainthearted. You have to work hard on maintaining a positive outlook when a problem is followed by another, and yet another," writes Lynette Clements, in "Growing Old is Not for the Fainthearted" (Medium.com, 16 Nov 2018). Clements quotes a New York Times article, "The Secret to Aging Well? Contentment," in which the author says, "Accept the uncertainties of old age without surrendering to them." Pretty good advice. You can't stop getting old if you keep on breathing, and in spite of best efforts to be healthy, diseases often ignore your preventatives and assault you anyway. As much as you'd like not to become one of those people whose night stands are covered with orange plastic bottles, doctors may tell you to take them anyway. (Rebel, I say!) Aging definitely isn't for the fainthearted.

Or as the author's daddy said in his last year of life (2004), "Growing old ain't for sissies."

Faith can (or will) move mountains

A question posed on Quora.com, where readers ask and readers answer, was this: "If faith can move mountains according to Jesus, then why is there no event in recorded history of a man doing so?" A reader who felt bold enough to type an answer did, asserting the belief that moving mountains is "absolutely possible," but never quite answering the question as it was put.[64]

An answer really wasn't necessary. The saying isn't meant to be taken as an implicit prediction that Mt. Everest will wind up in France one day. Rather, it is hyperbole, meaning that great things are possible when faith is applied.

The source is a saying of Jesus:

Matthew 17:20 "If ye have faith as a grain of mustard seed, ye shall say unto this mountain, Remove hence to yonder place; and it shall remove; and nothing shall be impossible unto you." *(See also Mark 11:23)*

The disciples had tried unsuccessfully to cast out a demon from someone's son. Jesus accomplished it and they asked him what their problem was. Lack of faith, was the answer. If their faith was only the size of a mustard seed, they could move mountains.

The phrase continues to be inspirational to Christians through the generations. It isn't said much outside Christian circles, but the occasional writer or speaker calls on the concept of the power of generic faith—essentially self-confidence.

Ben Raleigh wrote the words to "Faith Can Move Mountains," recorded by Johnnie Ray and the Four Lads in 1952 and more famously in 1954 by Nat King Cole. But

---

[64]*https://www.quora.com/If-faith-can-move-mountains-according-to-Jesus-then-why-is-there-n o-event-in-recorded-history-of-a-man-doing-so*

Raleigh's words were explicit in saying, "Darling, …I can move mountains if you have faith in me." God is not in the picture.

Less inspirational still is the comment of atheist William Gascoyne (slowly becoming famous), "I'm not convinced that faith can move mountains, but I've seen what it can do to skyscrapers." That was an allusion to the Twin Towers, taken down by Muslim terrorists on September 11, 2001. Gascoyne was taking "faith" in its more substantive sense—the Muslim faith—rather than the idea of confidence.

As off-base as the atheist's lampooning of Jesus' words is, it is less bizarre than some sociological researchers' seizure of the phrase. Consider just the title of a Research Gate article: "Faith Will Move Mountains: A Qualitative Exploration of Veiled British Muslim Women's Experiences in the UK Post-Brexit." What does that even mean?

Fortunately, the dominant use of the term continues to be an expression of belief that God can do anything and will do great things when people who believe in him express that belief toward specific goals—goals they believe are in God's will for them.

However, the tendency is for this faith to be ever so slightly trivialized by its commercialization (like Christmas), in that the saying, "Faith can move mountains," is available from thousands of retailers, emblazoned on hats, T-shirts, coffee mugs, tote bags, wall hangings and no end of other items. The makers of these things probably had faith they could make a mountain of money selling Jesus' words to the Christian public, and no doubt they have.

Fall from grace

This phrase originates with the Apostle Paul:

Galatians 5:4 "Christ is become of no effect unto you, whosoever of you are justified by the law; ye are fallen from grace."

In Christianity these Pauline words have two meanings, one in the Roman Catholic realm and one in the Protestant. The Catholic interpretation is that a Christian, by reverting to reliance on his own good behavior or by committing serious sins, can become unsaved again—lose eternal life.

Protestants abjured the power of church and priest to confer and control the grace of God. To most Protestants, "fall from grace" means that by becoming legalistic, they fall out of fellowship with God and stop experiencing the victory and joy that God's grace imparts. The author's initiation to seminary life in the 70s included becoming accustomed to the popular question as to whether he was "in the law" or "in grace." It was a juxtaposition of legalistic living versus freedom in Christ.

Anyway, neither meaning is exactly what the modern English speaker often tries to communicate by using the term. Instead, it has taken on the sense of losing esteem or position.

From the *Sunday Independent,* in Ireland: "Many of the men who have fallen from grace as a result of #MeToo [the anti-sexual-harassment movement launched on Twitter] wouldn't see themselves as sexual harassers in a million years."

One blogger typified falling from grace as merely losing fame, and noted that Winona Ryder's movie career plummeted after she was caught shoplifting.[65]

---

[65]*http://www.cracked.com/pictofacts-961-the-18-weirdest-ways-celebrities-have-fallen-from-grace/*

Fat of the land

Genesis 45:18 "And take your father and your households, and come unto me: and I will give you the good of the land of Egypt, and ye shall eat the fat of the land."

Like many of the phrases logged here in this book, "fat of the land" needs little if any explanation. But then, where would the book be?

The fat of an animal slaughtered for meat was where the flavor was—the good stuff! Anyone who knows anything about selecting a good steak knows to get one that has a decent amount of marbling in it—fat distributed throughout the meat. We trim excess fat from the edges of various cuts of meat sometimes, just to eliminate the added calories. But with some cuts—such as pork chops these days—cutting off the fat ensures that a meat cooked slowly will not be as tender or flavorful. The fat is where the taste is!

The fat of the land was a natural application of the idea. The Genesis 45 passage describes Pharaoh's invitation to Joseph's family in Canaan to escape the famine there by coming to Egypt and enjoying its plenty. If they had only known what lay ahead of them in a generation or two, they might have declined. Of course, it was all in God's plan to preserve them, even if through enslavement.

Modern usage is sometimes a recommendation for enjoyment and sometimes a condemnation of indolence. For instance, this comment from the New York Times about public opinions of food stamps: "Despite clear evidence to the contrary, the suspicion persists that many a recipient is living lazily off the fat of the land."[66] Jim Flynn disagrees. He thinks

---

[66]*New York Times*, 8/26/1982
(*https://www.nytimes.com/1982/08/26/opinion/living-off-the-fat-of-the-land.html*)

government itself is living off the fat of the land, by taxing us more and more heavily to fund anti-obesity programs.[67]

And then a *Science Daily* article borrows the phrase—have you noticed how often medical science picks up Bible terminology?—to describe the "strategy" of cancer cells, in this article title: "Living off the fat of the land: Do cancer cells synthesize parts for new cells or scavenge them from the environment?"[68]

And for yet another medical citation, "Living Off the Fat of the Land: Lipid Extraction Methods" was an August 1, 2015 article in LC GC Europe by Douglas E. Raynie about various ways to remove fats from substances.

A *Texas Monthly* article in 1976 conceived of diet and exercise gurus and weight-loss doctors as living off the fat of the land, quite literally. In the same vein, The *Pharma Letter* commented in 1994 that Interneuron Pharmaceuticals was living off the fat of the land with its dexfenfluramine, a drug for treating obesity. (Some of us would like a stock of it.)

There's even a community farm business called LOTFOTL (pronounced—yes, *pronounced*, lot-fot-uhl), which stands, obviously, for "Living Off the Fat of the Land." It's in Wisconsin. Its philosophy is: "To live harmoniously as a member of a greater community, to bask in your role in a system which feeds you so long as you feed it."[69]

---

[67]Jim Flynn, "Government is Living Off the Fat of the Land" (South Marion Citizen, 2/16/2012,

[68]Washington University in St. Louis. "Living off the fat of the land: Do cancer cells synthesize parts for new cells or scavenge them from the environment?." ScienceDaily. ScienceDaily, 31 March 2016. <www.sciencedaily.com/releases/2016/03/160331082845.htm>.

[69]*https://lotfotl.com/about/*

Fatted calf

It's a somewhat archaic form of description, but it works well and appears often, though mostly in the idiomatic sense.

Luke 15:30 "But as soon as this thy son was come, which hath devoured thy living with harlots, thou hast killed for him the fatted calf."

The brother of the Prodigal Son meant it quite literally when he complained that his daddy hadn't thrown any parties for him, but for his wastrel younger brother he had killed the animal who had been grazed luxuriously in preparation for slaughter.

More often than not these days, the expression is used of other indulgent preparations or provisions. But not always.

David Walls writes in *Avery Bishop: The Journey Home* (Xlibris Corp. 2012, page 42) about his homecoming. He described a church excited about the return: "They were all scurrying around like pets wanting to please their master. They killed the fatted calf for the event," he said. This author has partaken of quite a few fatted calves over the years in similar churches. Once in Texas it actually was a calf.

But PeTA thinks anyone who eats calf, or pig or chickens, or even chicken eggs, is immoral. They succeeded in pressuring Mepkin Abbey, a Trappist monastery in South Carolina, to stop its egg farm. The monks supported themselves partly from the proceeds. A PeTA writer on their site, peta.org, self-righteously says, "Holy men...need to be particularly accountable for cruel or unethical actions." Hmph! Eggs.

At any rate, someone commenting on the article on PeTA's site (in a comment PeTa deleted) said, "You *do* realize Jesus ate fish and had parables about meat meals like killing the fatted calf to welcome a prodigal son home?" Yeah, take *that*, PeTA!

Feet of clay

This phrase has been around a long time and has been applied to many, many, *many* people—and not just famous ones, either. Many children have been disappointed to find that their parents had feet of clay. Many spouses have made this discovery about their partners. And of course, the string of community, state, national and world leaders who have been caught in some shameful activity (See: "Fallen from grace") convinces most of us that everyone, absolutely everyone, has feet of clay.

And so we do. In everyday English the words mean that we are human. It's possible to think of this phrase as coming from the general teaching in Genesis that man was made from the earth. However, the exact phrase actually comes from a vision interpreted by Daniel:

Daniel 2: 31-33 "Thou, O king, sawest, and behold a great image. This great image, whose brightness was excellent, stood before thee; and the form thereof was terrible. This image's head was of fine gold, his breast and his arms of silver, his belly and his thighs of brass, His legs of iron, his feet part of iron and part of clay."

Three verses are included here because they explain what the partly clay feet were. Nebuchadnezzar, the king of Babylon, had a bad dream, and had ordered Daniel to tell him not only what his dream meant, but what it was in the first place. Daniel, up to the task in God's power, did so. The king had seen a beastly image that had, among other things, feet that were partly iron, partly clay. By way of interpretation, Daniel told Nebuchadnezzar this meant that the coming kingdom represented by the feet of both iron and clay would be partly strong and partly not: broken. The HCSB clarifies that the Hebrew for clay means fired clay, and that broken means brittle.

A person with feet of clay is someone who is typically human. Because of the context, the term usually refers to someone who has or still holds some position of prominence, if only to a small group like a family. And it's not a general descriptor. It gets put into use when that person has slipped and fallen, often on one of the temptations that are common to people in his or her profession or position. People in power are often tempted to take advantage of that power for sexual advantage. They also often fall prey to temptations to take bribes, etc. When they are discovered, then we say they have feet of clay. Truth is, they had those feet all along. They were vulnerable.

Willow Creek Community Church, the megachurch in northern Chicago, recently went through a difficult time regarding its founding pastor, Bill Hybels, who had become compromisingly involved with several women. When the news became known, the other pastors of the church resigned, mostly as they said for failing to hold Hybels accountable. It made a 2011 article by James Hamacher of the Richmond Baptist Association resonate loudly: "Bill has never hid the fact that he has feet of clay and often makes huge mistakes."[70] Indeed.

Not everyone reserves the phrase for career-ending sins. To one blogger, John McCain had feet of clay, merely for not being an ultra-conservative. And Elon Musk has feet of clay for having shot his red Tesla convertible into space, where he lost control of it and it drifted into the great beyond.

---

[70]Jim Hamacher, "The clay feet club" (*https://www.mdba.org/the-clay-feet-club*, 8/22/2011)

Fell by the wayside

Usually spelled as one word in English, "way side" is two in the KJV in the source of this idiom:

Matthew 13:4 "And when he sowed, some seeds fell by the way side, and the fowls came and devoured them up."

Jesus' parable of the soils or the sower (See also: Fell on stony ground) was about how poorly or well seed germinates and produces a crop—an object lesson about people responding to the word of God. The first seed cast fell "by the wayside," or the path, hardened and packed down by frequent passage of feet. Accordingly, the seed didn't get in the soil and didn't germinate.

The idiom this phrase constitutes in modern English means one's efforts are useless or wasted, because nothing will come of them.

Unfortunately, "fall by the wayside" has become a fuzzy, loose term for failure, a development that weakens its best meaning.

The Longman Dictionary of Common English itself contributes to this loose meaning when it gives as an example of the idiom, "A lot of marriages fall by the wayside because couples cannot talk to each other."

So did Yahoo (China) in reporting that "Many party stalwarts fell by the wayside on election day." We suppose that means the candidates lost. That wayside is getting crowded.

And *The Independent* in the UK reported that a program created in Britain to win the war on drugs there had been redirected, watered down, shuffled around, and finally "fallen by the wayside." Let's stay out of the wayside. Too many abject failures there.

Fell on his sword

1 Samuel 31:4 "Then said Saul unto his armourbearer, Draw thy sword, and thrust me through therewith; lest these uncircumcised come and thrust me through, and abuse me. But his armourbearer would not; for he was sore afraid. Therefore Saul took a sword, and fell upon it."

It is worth noting that Saul had already been wounded by arrows. It is also worth noting that after Saul fell on his sword, so did his armorbearer.

Falling on one's own sword, literally, was a gruesome but nonetheless occasionally encountered act of a soldier in the field in ancient times. According to The Helen, by Euripides, Ajax fell on his own sword at Troy when a rival won Helen and he was about to be disgraced. French Admiral Villeneuve under Napolean was responsible for losses that finally shamed him to the point that he committed suicide, according to some reports by falling on his own sword.

The actual act is rarer these days because in most cultures the idea that personal honor is worth suicide has fallen into disfavor — an improvement, in our opinion. However, the concept that people should metaphorically fall on their own swords for the good of their organizations or causes is still very much alive. It's an idiomatic expression for what is sometimes — and very much less dramatically — called "taking one for the team."

A blogger describes Marco Rubio's actions in the 2016 presidential campaign, where he won enough delegates to hurt Donald Trump's chances in the party primary. Says *dajeeps*, "Rubio exits on his own sword," and later that "he fell" on it. Politics is dangerous business, win or lose.

Menzies Campbell, a UK liberal party head a few years back, abruptly resigned in the face of sharply declining polls. A senior party source said, "He told them he had decided to go. He decided to put the party's interests before his own. It was an honourable man doing the honourable thing. Effectively it was a bloodless coup. It was not 'et tu Brute.' He fell on his own sword."[71] The Brits often use far more words than required. The source could have said simply that Campbell quit for the good of the party. More political death.

And talk about taking one for the team: "The knives for Roy Barreto had long been sharpened, but on Tuesday he fell on his own sword. The Orlando Pirates coach left the club's Parktown, Johannesburg, offices sans his job, his pride and, perhaps more strikingly, even his black-and-white tracksuits." So wrote Nkareng Matshe in the IOL, in 2003 about the voluntary exodus of his soccer team in South Africa.[72] He had a bad record, things were getting tight in the clubhouse, and he had heard rumors he was going to get canned anyway. Falling on his own sword made it look more like he was taking one for the team than that he was escaping by the skin of his teeth (See: Skin of one's teeth).

---

[71]Michael Settle, "He fell on his own sword" (*The Herald* (UK), 16 Oct 2007)

[72]Nkareng Matshe, "Pirates' boss Baretto jumps ship" (IOL, 22 Oct 2003, https://www.iol.co.za/capeargus/sport/pirates-boss-barreto-jumps-ship-529634) 4 Jan 2019

Fell on stony ground

This idiom means something very similar to "fell on deaf ears:" to be ignored or rejected, to fail to be productive.

Mark 4:5 "And some fell on stony ground, where it had not much earth; and immediately it sprang up, because it had no depth of earth."

When Jesus told the parable of the soils, some seed fell where nothing took root, some on plowed ground ready for planting, and some "fell on stony ground." This was a typical kind of terrain in Israel, where there was a thin layer of topsoil covering rock. Seed falling there might spring up rapidly in warm dirt, but die when it couldn't really put down roots. By this image Jesus intended to communicate the idea that the word of God comes to some people who receive it with vacant enthusiasm and ultimately abandon it, never having let themselves respond to it deeply. In other words, shallow.

Today's use of the phrase generally lacks the element of an initial, enthusiastic response. It skips directly to the idea of being ignored or rejected.

Olaf Storbeck described in a 24 May 2016 Reuters article Bayer Corporation's $62 billion bid for U.S. Seed maker Monsanto." As Storbeck said of the negative reaction, "Bayer's synergy hopes fall on stony ground."

And in the blog "Howling For Justice" for the gray wolf, the writer bemoans the fact that "the words of passionate wolf advocates who attended the meeting and spoke out for wolves, "fell on stony ground."[73] Wolves can't get a break these days.

---

[73]https://howlingforjustice.wordpress.com/2012/03/24/wolf-advocates-pleas-to-idfg-commissioners-fall-on-stony-ground/

Fight the good fight

Aussie Lucy Richards described a work transition this way: "The invaluable lessons about tools and processes I learned while fumbling my way through the agency-speak inspired me to hastily jump off the corporate hamster wheel and into the equally complex, yet more meaningful (to me, at least) world of global health." After a re-reading, Richards' own "agency speak" might make sense. Anyway, the title she gave this entry on her blog, "Global Health" *(https://blogs.plos.org/ global health/2018/07/using-tech-to-fight-the-good-fight/)* was "Using tech to fight the good fight." Ah, how the mighty have fallen (See: How the mighty have fallen).

It used to be, when this phrase was coined by translation of those precise Greek words from Paul, that it meant a life lived for Jesus Christ by faith:

1 Timothy 6:12 "Fight the good fight of faith, lay hold on eternal life, whereunto thou art also called, and hast professed a good profession before many witnesses."

"Fight the good fight," like most inspirational phrases from the Bible, has made it into hymn, song, album and book titles too many to name. Most of these are Christian oriented, as might be assumed. We suppose that the words are not so proprietary to the Christian faith or the Bible that they may not legitimately be used to refer to any worthy struggle for good goals. And that's what it means in today's English.

The Guardian titles a piece looking for your donations, "Fight the good fight." Says the editor, "Our journalism remains open and accessible to everyone and with your help we can keep it that way."[74] Free speech should be free. We agree. So, no, we

---

[74]Unsigned editorial, *The Guardian, 13 Apr 2006* (https://www.theguardian.com/ commentisfree/2006/apr/14/religion.comment) 4 Jan 2019

won't pay for it.

Fight the Good Fight is the name of a CrossFit fitness organization. It fits.

And, Fight the Good Fight Foundation is a nonprofit organization that helps build safe houses for victims of human trafficking.

But we're not sure how good the fight always is. It depends on your definition of "good." Ann Reid, new head of the advocacy group the National Center for Science Education "promises to 'fight the good fight' against attacks on evolution and climate change in U.S. classrooms." That means she plans to butt heads with people who object to teaching evolution as the only possible explanation of origins, and with opponents of the wholesale preaching of "global warming" as caused by human beings. The latter makes our own blood boil.

Filthy lucre

This quaint expression comes from Latin via French. The King James scholars used it to translate a compact word in Greek, *aischrokerdeis*, which means greedy of dishonest gain. It appears in Paul's first letter to Timothy:

1 Timothy 3:8 "Likewise must the deacons be grave, not doubletongued, not given to much wine, not greedy of filthy lucre."

The word shows up again in Titus where similar instructions are given. It's surprising, given the Pauline instruction, how many people have ignored it. Many televangelists and some religious entertainers might debate whether the millions they rake in are "dishonest," which is inherent in the meaning of the word, but it would be hard to argue that representing a ministry as existing to tell the gospel of Christ and minister to people around the country and the world, but then siphoning off a goodly portion of offerings for lavish possessions, can be anything but dishonest, even perhaps if it's done in the open.

But we digress. Anyway, in Christian circles "filthy lucre" is most often found as a synonym for money, in general, whether dishonestly gained or not. Some Christians can't escape thinking that money itself is evil (See: Love of money).

Molly Crabapple *(https://www.vice.com/en_us/article/mvp8dn/filthy-lucre)* writes in the bitterest terms about her experience of trying to be a successful artist in America, thinking her enemy is the economic system under which this great country operates. She laments that "it's near impossible to live the average American dream on the average American salary." She complains about bonuses given to people who are already rich. But she finally gives in to the system, realizing that "being an artist means you're in thrall to cash."

Nevertheless, her entire diatribe was prefaced by, and

overshadowed by, the lengthy description of some people of great means who fly Virgin Upper Class out of Heathrow, who scarcely touch the great unwashed who fly any other class. Molly is mostly obsessed with the fact that some people have a lot of money and that some people don't. The title of her article, simply "Filthy Lucre," gives away her equivalency. To her it's the same as "filthy rich," and she hates, utterly hates it. And loves it. And wishes she had more of it.

Artist Darren Waterston apparently has a different view of the art world. In an article by Philip Kennicott entitled "Filthy Lucre and the complicated relationship between artist and buyer," Kennicott examines a work by Waterston parodying Whistler's Peacock Room, an actual room decorated in mural art. In Waterston's version it's a bizarre complex of broken, misaligned imperfection.

Kennicott describes how Waterston's work was at auction the morning after "an overhyped Picasso sold in New York for $179 million, setting a record for a painting sold at auction." Kennicott juxtaposed the two as if to say that "Filthy Lucre" is Waterston's illustration of the "absurd excesses"[75] of the art world. So for one artist, "filthy lucre" is the regrettable means of her success, while for another it's the enemy of art itself.

Meanwhile, on St. John's Antigua, the MP for Barbuda, Trevor Walker, "complained that the voting list was still tainted and that there was 'filthy lucre' being circulated during the campaign that he claimed 'changed the whole dynamics and context' of the local elections."[76] There's nowhere in the world where elections aren't for sale.

---

[75]https://www.washingtonpost.com/entertainment/museums/filthy-lucre-and-the-com plicated-relationship-between-artist-and-buyer/2015/05/19/96628198-fd7c-11e4-8b6c-0dcce21 e223d_story.html?utm_term=.7e824409565f.

[76]In *The Daily Observer* (https://antiguaobserver.com/filthy-lucre/) 4 Jan 2019.

Fire and brimstone

Sometimes it's "hellfire and brimstone." Most often heard as a description of a certain kind of preacher, "fire and brimstone" evokes images of the energetic, delivery of impassioned histrionics. Typically, such preaching would look and sound like that, but actually the fire and brimstone in the expression do not refer to the preacher's style but rather to his message:

Genesis 19: 24-26 - "Then the LORD rained upon Sodom and upon Gomorrah brimstone and fire from the LORD out of heaven."

Fire and brimstone are images of coming judgment that call upon the actual incidence of fire and brimstone that destroyed Sodom and Gomorrah. Theologians debate what the judgment on those cities actually consisted of (because debate is what theologians do best), but whatever its source and chemical composition, it was sufficient to do the job.[77] Preachers sometimes look into the possibly near future to proclaim God's judgment on the earth in connection with the second coming of Jesus Christ prophesied throughout the New Testament.

The phrase appears in Revelation 9:18 where John describes the sixth angel in his vision, who loosed 200 million horsemen, whose animals breathed "fire and smoke and brimstone." Brimstone is burning sulfur, very difficult to extinguish, and therefore an apt image for a never-ending hell.

The Psalmist also employed this frightening image in Psalm 11:6. It seems the Bible's symbols for final judgment on sin are unwaveringly, unmitigatedly bad. See John 3:16 for the fire extinguisher.

---

[77]The skeptic should read the article at https://www.lifesitenews.com/news/archeologists-sodom-and-gomorrah-literally-destroyed-by-fire-and-brimstone before dismissing the biblical description as metaphorical or fictional.

The phrase isn't always used for specific teaching about eternal realities, but sometimes as a general warning about God's disapproval. A newspaper covered a community pastor's "fire and brimstone sermon" given the Sunday after the newspaper had reported that the corner market next door to the preacher's house had applied for a license to sell beer.

Always looking to lighten the mood and create a diversion from the eternal realities, secular society comes up with whimsical creations such as Fire and Brimstone Cocktails, made with apple cider, Jack Daniels Tennessee Fire cinnamon whiskey and other ingredients. And some entrepreneur established Fire and Brimstone Tavern in Alpharetta, Georgia, described as "a gastropub/sports bar." It features lots of locally brewed beers, liquor, and a hookah and cigar lounge. If the eternal realities were nothing more than drinks and cigars, the patrons of this tavern would have little to worry about.

Billy Graham, whom most of the world still recognizes as the most prominent preacher and evangelist of the 20th century (he rose to fame in Los Angeles in 1949, the year of this author's birth), spoke early and often of hell. Over the years he didn't always try to communicate the nature of hell as a place of real fire and brimstone, but he never wavered as to its reality. In his final book, *Where I Am*, Graham wrote: ""I can say with certainty that if there is no literal fire in Hell, then God is using symbolic language to indicate something far worse."[78]

---

[78]Billy Graham, *Where I Am: Heaven, Eternity and Our Life Beyond* (Nashville, Thomas Nelson, 2015).

Fleshpots

We're not sure how many other writings contemporary with the production of the King James Version of the Bible contained the word "fleshpot," but its survival to the present is certainly attributable to the KJV. It comes from Exodus:

Exodus 16:3 "…Would to God we had died by the hand of the LORD in the land of Egypt, when we sat by the flesh pots, and when we did eat bread to the full…"

A fleshpot was just that, a pot in which meat was cooked. Today it might be the fryer at Kentucky Fried Chicken. For the Israelites wandering out into the desert of Sinai, conjuring up the image of those kettles they left when they escaped slavery in Egypt provoked their complaint to Moses.

Today, the term is used whimsically to describe restaurants and comfortable living. But something about the sound of the word has spawned seedy misuse.

Fleshpot on 42nd Street is a grindhouse movie by Andy Milligan, of a genre this author would not go to see. The title is a complete misconstrual of the word, probably intentional, and appears to be an amalgam of flesh and sexpot, which pretty much describes what the film appears to be about, from its description. No footnote gives an online location. Readers don't need to waste their time.

In the same vein, *Fleshpots of Antiquity: the Lives and Loves of Ancient Courtesans* is a book by Henry Frichet, who likewise thinks the word has a sexual meaning.

Back on the more reputable side of the tracks, "Fleshpots in Egypt" is the name of a bluegrass band that says of itself that it's how Lutheran hymns would sound if the Reformation had begun in Appalachia.

Fly in the ointment

A deputy took a sandwich from home for his lunch and warmed it in a convenience store microwave. His new partner asked him why he didn't just get one of the store's very good sandwiches. The deputy's face turned serious. He never ate fast food because once had got a sandwich with a hair in it!

Well, most of us don't like foreign objects in our food, and the sight of one usually prompts us to throw the whole thing away. We might adopt the philosophy of the waiter called to a table over a complaint of a fly in his soup. The waiter's response was, "Don't worry, he won't eat much."

Apparently, some substances fair more poorly when adulterated by such things as dead insects. We get "fly in the ointment" from the Bible:

Ecclesiastes 10:1 "Dead flies cause the ointment of the apothecary to send forth a stinking savour: so doth a little folly him that is in reputation for wisdom and honour."

For the writer of Ecclesiastes, the remark about the fly was an illustration; the important part of the verse was about a man's reputation being ruined by a little bit of foolishness. The part of the verse that passed into everyday English vernacular was about the fly, of course, not the foolishness.

The idiom commonly means something seemingly small that ruins something much more significant or valuable.

Perhaps it wasn't so small a flaw that one commenter thought would ruin Mexico's 2018 proposal to establish a free zone along their side of the border with the U.S. "Big fly in the ointment: Those people coming to the US illegally are not [in the] upstanding, taxpaying, working class in Mexico."

Forbidden Fruit

Ask people where this idiom came from and many will know it's the Bible story of Adam and Eve. Ask them what the forbidden fruit was and aside from the many who say it was an apple, many others will say it was *sex!*

The latter interpretation is wrong on every level, but it persists. As to an apple's being the fruit, the story of Adam and Eve in the garden of Eden describes the pair's eating the actual fruit of the tree in the middle of the garden, but it doesn't identify the fruit. Since the fruit was forbidden to them, identification of it may be impossible because it's likely that it doesn't exist in today's world.

Genesis 2:17 "But of the tree of the knowledge of good and evil, thou shalt not eat of it: for in the day that thou eatest thereof thou shalt surely die."

Even for those who take the story as history, Eden is *also* symbolic, like many other stories in the Bible. To make a long story short, forbidden fruit represents anything you might want but God says "no" to. Since God created the tree, the restricted thing is good in itself—just not for you.

In translation to the present day, the idiom means any disallowed pleasure, but one that by its very nature, or simply because it *is* disallowed, is intensely desired.

The fruit may not be *only* sex, *but*—on NBC's "Chicago PD," Officer Kim Burgess thought Sgt. Trudy Platt was going to scold her for having a romance with someone in the district house. Sgt. Platt surprised her with candid advice: "Why don't you have fun while you're young? God knows I've tasted my share of forbidden district-house fruit over the years."[79]

---

[79]"At Least It's Justice," *Chicago PD*, s01e10, NBC.

For ever and ever

Appearing in both the Old and New Testaments, this phrase is perhaps most memorable from the last book:

Revelation 7:12 "Amen: Blessing, and glory, and wisdom, and thanksgiving, and honour, and power, and might, be unto our God for ever and ever. Amen."

We who have sung in Handel's Messiah are familiar with the transition from the penultimate number, "Worthy is the Lamb" to the ultimate one, "Amen." The bridge is the grand chorus singing resolutely and slowly, "For ever and ever!" For those of you who have never heard these two numbers together and who've always heard only selections from the Messiah ending with the Hallelujah Chorus, you've missed a treat. For those of you who've never heard the Messiah, shame on you.

Anyway, the meaning of for ever and ever, or forever and ever, is just that. There's nothing idiomatic here, just a phrase illustrating the concept of eternity. One "ever" would have done it; the "illustration" part comes in the repetition. We could go on: forever and ever and ever. Randy Travis did, in his song "Forever and ever, Amen."

Of course, the phrase is also used lightly: Engagement rings are forever and ever (except that they're not); land is forever (uh, close but no cigar); a photographer advertises forever and ever images (in your Kodachrome or digital dreams); Forever and Ever is the name of artist Greg Olsen's website—we like his paintings with Christian themes, but they won't last *that* long; and Forever and Ever is the name of a floral arrangement by Forever My Dahhhlin florist—and if you've found a way to make roses last more than a couple of weeks at the most, please tell us. It will make Valentine's Day much better!

Four corners of the earth

Isaiah 11:12 "And he shall set up an ensign for the nations, and shall assemble the outcasts of Israel, and gather together the dispersed of Judah from the four corners of the earth."

Isaiah was written about the same time as the Greek myth describing how the Titans hold up the four corners of heaven and the earth. In this cosmology the earth was flat. But Isaiah wasn't teaching errant cosmology; he was using a popular idiom to mean "as far as you might go." The Jews, dispersed to the four corners of the earth, would be reassembled.

According to the Flat Earth Society, Brimstone Head on Fogo Island is one of the four corners of the earth.[80] So far, nobody has gone there and fallen off.

Apparently, however, it doesn't bother Computerworld, writing about a cellular device—which operates of course on cell towers, which communicate with satellites, which revolve around a *spherical* earth—to say the device could reach "the four corners of the earth." (See *https://www.computerworld.com /article/3093025/networking/facebook-device-could-bring-internet-to-four-corners-of-the-earth.html* for details.)

Oh, and the Four Corners of the Earth is also a sandwich place in Burlington, VT. It appears to be as much about beer as sandwiches. The Titans get thirsty out there holding up those corners.

The only four corners we know about personally are those of Arizona, Utah, Colorado, and New Mexico, where they come together. Cool! Actually, no, it's really hot. It's in the desert, after all.

---

[80]http://www.freecandie.com/2012/09/i-went-to-one-of-the-four-corners-of-the-world/

Gird your loins

Men in Bible times usually wore flowing robes of mid calf length. To run, they had to pull the skirt through their knees to the back, separate it around the waist and tie it in the front. That was called girding up the loins.

1 Kings 18:46 "And the hand of the LORD was on Elijah; and he girded up his loins, and ran before Ahab to the entrance of Jezreel."

In 2008 Joe Biden advised a campaign crowd to "gird your loins," since the tasks ahead for the next president would be "like cleaning the Augean stables." Aside from the mixed metaphors, he meant simply to "brace themselves for a test of mental or emotional endurance."[81]

This phrase from the Bible doesn't get much use in the modern world except by people who are intentionally quoting the Bible when they say it. We included it here because it won a coin toss.

---

[81]Juliet Lapidos, "Loin-Girding 101" (http://www.slate.com/articles/news_and_politics/explainer/2008/10/loingirding_101.html).

Give up the ghost

Job was in a funk after Satan had gotten permission to make his life miserable and had begun doing so. When friends showed up to commiserate, he told them how depressed he was, and he used a memorable biblical phrase for "dying."

Job 3:11 "Why died I not from the womb? why did I not give up the ghost when I came out of the belly?"

Like George Bailey in *It's a Wonderful Life*, Job wished he had never been born. Barring that, he wished he had died when he was delivered. He was really low.

The phrase appears numerous times in scripture, including John's statement that Jesus on the cross "gave up the ghost." Modern versions say "spirit" instead of ghost; the concept is that at death the spirit leaves the body.

While these days you do find some references to people giving up the ghost, most of the time it will be a description of some non-living thing.

A short story, "Gave Up the Ghost," inspired a movie about a writer whose computer dies and takes with it his novel in progress. A repairman suggests summoning the ghost of the computer to recover it. Well, if *deus machina*, then maybe...

Best Buy used to be a thriving electronics store, but a few years ago, according to several writers, they gave up the ghost.

A well pump gave up the ghost. Your car gave up the ghost. According to the UK's *Government Gazette*, even British industry gave up the ghost, somewhere in the past fifty years.

Spaceflight Now even says that the Hubble Telescope has found that the old star NGC 6369 in the Little Ghost Nebula, has given up the ghost. Considering the fact that NGC 6369 is as many as 30 quadrillion miles away, it must have died about 5,000 years ago. Rest in peace.

Go the extra mile

Mark Twain used to say he was in the Bible:

Matthew 5:41 "And whosoever shall compel thee to go a mile, go with him twain." (Go with him, Twain!)

A Roman soldier could compel a subject to carry his pack a mile. Jesus called for his followers to show their servant spirit and willingly give more than was required. (And in doing so, they would also heap flaming coals on their heads—another biblical idiom.)

Modern English speakers have updated the form but retained the sense: Go the second mile. Usually it is employed in all seriousness.

A pharmacist ignores regular business hours and does what's necessary to fill emergency prescriptions, even delivering them himself in the dead of night or in frigid temps, whatever it takes to serve his community. The Rotary Club gives him the Second Mile Award.

As with the story of the pharmacist, most references to "going the second mile" are to how people give 110%, so to speak, doing what they were already motivated to do. However, the thrust of Jesus' exhortation was to continue to do willingly what one is required to do initially. Giving extra money to the government on top of your taxes might qualify.

Yeah, no.

God speed

In *Star Wars: The Last Jedi,* Vice Admiral Holdo wishes the fighters, "God speed," leaving many fans of the film franchise wondering what happened to "May the force be with you." Apparently it was a nod to a longstanding tradition of appealing to God for the success of military endeavors.

2 John 1:11 "If there come any unto you, and bring not this doctrine, receive him not into your house, neither bid him God speed."

The translation "God speed" is not exact. The Greek word literally means to rejoice. A closer translation today might be, "Have a nice day!" But in King James's day, "God speed" was an expression meaning pretty much the same thing, a sort of all-purpose well-wishing like the Hebrew "shalom."

Along the way, God speed (or "God's speed) became a traditional wish imparted to many official endeavors. In February 1962 John Glenn got into a capsule atop a rocket and prepared to be blasted into space for the first time an American would orbit the earth. Today we can hear the audio recording of his colleagues in Mission Control saying to him through his helmet radio, "In God's speed, John Glenn." Since then, NASA has regularly repeated the blessing when men and women have ascended the gantry and been sealed into a capsule or shuttle.

Kind of outshines, "Have a nice day," doesn't it?

God forbid

References to God often run afoul of the prohibition of taking his name in vain (Exodus 20:7), and this one sometimes does. To invoke the name of God when one really doesn't mean to call upon God is empty (vain) and unworthy. However, sometimes it is a valid invocation, as in:

Genesis 44:7 "And they said unto him, Wherefore saith my lord these words? God forbid that thy servants should do according to this thing."

Bible figures sometimes appealed to the grace of God to keep them from acting a certain way, or to prevent terrible things happening to them. To say, "God forbid," can be a two-word prayer.

Paul breathed such a prayer in Romans 3:3-4: "For what if some did not believe? shall their unbelief make the faith of God without effect? God forbid!"

Sometimes it's an interjection, as from this comment on a website: "He can afford the best cars for them as a father whom God has blessed. Is it when they are involved in a tricycle accident (God forbid) that he will now buy them cars to drive without legs or hands?" (It was a very strange article.)

Sometimes it really doesn't seem to make sense when it's used, as in a piece contending that "Israel must accept that the U.S. will no longer police the Middle East:" "...The failed architects of the wars in the Greater Middle East ...are trying to drag the United States into a new military adventure in Syria. And God forbid, that idiot occupying the White House refuses to buy the goods. What a Chutzpah!" We're not sure what function "God forbid" has in the remark, unless it were to render it sarcastic.

God knows

Here's another expression from the Bible often used with less than holy intentions.

2 Corinthians 12:2-3 "I knew such a man, (whether in the body, or out of the body, I cannot tell: God knoweth."

Paul literally meant that he didn't know but that God did. It was a purposeful affirmation of the omniscience of God. We don't say, "knoweth," anymore, but plenty of people say, "God knows," merely as an intensifier of whatever else they're about to say.

"We hardly ever saw eye to eye on the same things," writes Ms. Mary Louise in *When Love is Blind: from Hurt to Healing,* "but he wouldn't let me leave him, and God knows I tried on many occasions." God does, indeed, know, but Mary Louise wasn't making any theological statement. It was in vain.

"God knows I didn't mean to fall in love with her," wrote Ernest Hemingway in *A Farewell to Arms.* Papa, too, used the phrase mostly to intensify his claim, as if swearing to its truth by invoking the Almighty.

And then there's the claim of Vicky Pagaria, in her book, *Magic of Love:* "God knows I did not want her to marry that jerk, but Maya was right that she had to decide for herself." Now, if only Maya knew what God knows.

Finally, there's the assertion of a nameless, blogging retiree in "Chasing After Paradise" who writes, "I decided that rather than go back onto the job market and end up God knows where doing God knows what, I'd go back to the old stomping grounds." Here, the phrase is equivalent to, "I don't know." Which takes us back to Paul's use of it to the Corinthians.

Good old age

"In spite of his bad constitution, his gluttonous habits and the conflicting treatment of his three chief physicians, Louis XIV, lived to the good old age of 77," so says M. Le Roi, the Librarian of Versailles. This expression has been around a long time. It was memorialized in the KJV as a translation of the Hebrew of the Old Testament.

Genesis 25:8 "Then Abraham gave up the ghost, and died in a good old age, an old man, and full of years; and was gathered to his people."

Other scriptures also use the expression.

It might be generalized that most people would like to attain a good old age before they died. Few people dream of dying young. However, most people would put the emphasis on *good*. Some sources employing the term focus on what would make growing old good, or at least not so bad.

In an abstract of their article, "A Good Old Age: Paradox or Possibility," authors Margaret Gatz and Stephen H. Zarit say, "How do we assure that we will have a good old age, by any definition? We turn to mental health theorists to elaborate our definition of life satisfaction and well-being and then to psychological research to suggest how to prepare ourselves now for a good old age in the future."[82]

To Robert Roush, "Exercise may be the key." Roush says, "I've never met any one who wouldn't want to have a good old age, and since the title implies that attaining this goal is a possibility, just maybe you can."[83]

---

[82]Gatz, M., & Zarit, S. H. (1999). "A good old age: Paradox or possibility." In V. L. Bengtson & K. W. Schaie (Eds.), Handbook of theories of aging (pp. 396-416). New York, NY, US: Springer Publishing Co.

[83](https://www.bcm.edu/centers/huffington-center-on-aging/community/a-good-old-age)

Good Samaritan

Like "Prodigal Son," the phrase "Good Samaritan" is not in the Bible, but the good Samaritan himself is.

Luke 10:30-37 "But a certain Samaritan, as he journeyed, came where he was: and when he saw him, he had compassion on him."

What makes the Samaritan good is that he stopped to help his Jewish neighbor when the man's own countrymen—a priest and a Levite, no less—didn't. That was the point of the parable, which Jesus offered in answer to the question, "Who is my neighbor." The response was obviously, "The question is not who your neighbor is, but to whom are you a neighbor." That's what makes a good Samaritan.

There are numerous Good Samaritan hospitals around the country, as well as Good Samaritan funds of various organizations, and a host of Good Samaritan laws in states (most of these laws protect people who stop to help accident victims from being sued afterwards).

In the news, a January 2, 2019 shoplifting incident in Loomis, CA, led to a violent encounter with security in which the perpetrators began stabbing security personnel. About that time, a good guy in a truck nearby who had a firearm got out and got involved. Police said, "Good Samaritan drew his firearm, told the second suspect, the female, to drop her knife, which she did. He kept her from picking it back up until law enforcement arrived." More evidence that the solution to a bad guy with a gun is a good guy with a gun.

Hard hearted

"Hard hearted" derives from one of the many variations on "harden his heart," chiefly found in the Old Testament. While possibly not unique to the Bible, the phrase did enter the English language through the influence of the Scriptures.

Matthew 19:8 "He saith unto them, Moses because of the hardness of your hearts suffered you to put away your wives: but from the beginning it was not so."

This New Testament example of a heart being hard is the closest to the sense the phrase is usually given today. Jesus said the Israelites were hard of heart because they were resistant to the higher law of love—which might have preserved marriages—and chose instead to divorce for just about any cause.

The Old Testament mentions various persons with hard hearts, notably Pharaoh, who repeatedly responded to the ten plagues invoked by Moses by promising to let the Hebrew slaves go, and then he changed his mind. Sometimes Exodus says Pharaoh hardened his own heart, and then it says that God hardened it. Both are true.

"Well a hard headed woman / A soft hearted man / Been the cause of trouble / Ever since the world began" sang Elvis Presley.

Sometimes it's the other way around. The *Los Angeles Times* hates Donald Trump and refers to his "hard-hearted immigration policies." Another newspaper calls Democrats the soft-hearted Mommy Party. Perspective is everything.

He who lives by the sword, dies by the sword

Also expressed in the imperative, "Live by the sword, die by the sword," these words come from Jesus' lips:

Matthew 26:52 "Then said Jesus unto him, Put up again thy sword into his place: for all they that take the sword shall perish with the sword."

Peter the disciple attempted to defend Jesus from being arrested. Jesus was rebuking him, and creating an idiom.

The Independent Irish News reporting on the fatal shooting of John Gilligan, a notorious drug trafficker, said that people in the community commenting on it expressed sympathy for Gilligan's brother, but none for him. "Live by the sword, die by the sword," they said.

An editorial comment in *The Union* (Nevada County, CA) said in 2008, "The same administration that did not see fit to fund health insurance for every child in America wants to come to the rescue of Wall Street to the tune of 700 billion dollars. My thought is 'live by the sword, die by the sword.'" Another editorialist nine years later remarked about the complaint that President Trump was undoing the Obama legacy, "It's just 'live by the executive order, die by the executive order.'"

A Mafia hit man is suspected of killing FBI informant "Whitey" Bulger in a West Virginia prison October 30, 2018. Whitey was in jail for thirty-two counts of racketeering and complicity (at the very least) in nineteen murders. His demise was no surprise. And while even the murder of a multiple murderer is still a crime, it was still a fitting end. Live by the sword—well, you know.

Head on a platter

When someone wants to describe a sudden comeuppance carried out with extreme prejudice, he may say someone has been handed his head on a platter. The expression comes from the gospels. The provocative daughter of Herodius excited King Herod so much with her dancing that he promised to give her anything she wanted. Herodius, Herod's brother Philip's wife—who was incensed by John the Baptist's condemnation of her for marrying Herod—told her daughter to ask for John's head on a platter. Herod was drunk, but he had promised. He sent an executioner, who beheaded John:

Mark 6:28 "And brought his head in a charger, and gave it to the damsel: and the damsel gave it to her mother."

Americans haven't said "charger" for a long time. "Platter" replaced the word in the expression. The ASV has "platter" as early as 1901.

Fashionista magazine said that "i-D magazine serves Lara Stone's head on a platter in its upcoming Q&A issue."[84] Stone is a "supermodel." What in the world did she do to deserve such treatment? Trip on the runway?

Columnist Russell Turner used the phrase in 2015 in regard to Republicans who wouldn't overturn President Obama's Affordable Care Act. Turner gave an illustration: "If for some reason a coach or a player doesn't give his all the fans quickly demand their head on a platter. Sports fans are very unforgiving when it comes to their sporting events when the team members are uninspired."[85] The 2016 electorate may have been the executioner Turner was waiting for.

---

[84](https://fashionista.com/2013/03/lara-stones-head-gets-served-on-a-platter-carla-bruni-returns-to-modeling-and-american-eagle-creates-the-skinniest-skinny-jeans-ever)
[85](https://www.reddirtreport.com/prairie-opinions/conservative-view-head-platter)

Hold your peace

This expression survives in modern English mostly in artistic works, books, television and movie titles, and, of course, in the typical but somewhat archaic wedding ceremony: "If any man may show just cause why these two should not be joined together, let him speak now, or forever hold his peace." We know of a dozen or so instances in which somebody actually did. Sometimes it made a difference, sometimes not.

2 Kings 2:5 "And the sons of the prophets that were at Jericho came to Elisha, and said unto him, Knowest thou that the LORD will take away thy master from thy head to day? And he answered, Yea, I know it; hold ye your peace."

When Elisha said it to the "sons of the prophets" (sort of ancient seminary students), it was a polite way of saying that Elijah's impending departure was not going to be debated, dissected, deliberated, or even discussed. Just be quiet about it. Wait, and wait silently.

When Mordecai said it to Esther, he was urging her *not* to be quiet: "For if thou altogether holdest thy peace at this time, then shall there enlargement and deliverance arise to the Jews from another place; but thou and thy father's house shall be destroyed: and who knoweth whether thou art come to the kingdom for such a time as this?" Speak! Speak now!

In *Chicken Soup for the Soul; Teens Talk High School* (2008), Carol E. Ayer wrote about her terrifying first experience of public speaking. Quoting first the Bible and then André Gide, she said the lesson she learned was "Speak now or forever hold your peace; there are very few monsters who warrant the fear we have of them."

Holier than thou

One of the more irritating insults non-church people hurl at church folks who simply try to share their beliefs is that Christians are "holier than thou." Almost without exception these days, this expression is a criticism, not a compliment.

It started out that way, too. Through the prophet Isaiah, God raked over the coals the Israelites who had developed extensive and elaborate rituals of consecration but who were nothing of the sort in their actual lives.

Isaiah 65:5 "Which say, Stand by thyself, come not near to me; for I am holier than thou. These are a smoke in my nose, a fire that burneth all the day."

The ones who said, "I am holier than thou," were the "holy" men, and they said it to everyone else. God saw it all and was wroth. That's a good Bible word for really, *really angry!*

There's usually little the Christian can do to fend off the accusation of being "holier than thou." Often it simply isn't true, but it's really an insult that acts like a wall being erected to defend against Christian witness. The accuser isn't interested in being set straight on the Christian's actual character.

It isn't always used in connection with religious people being hypocritical. Politicians trade barbs with the accusation now and then. When President Trump nominated Brett Kavanaugh to the Supreme Court and Democrats almost uniformly opposed him tooth and nail, Trump accused them of being holier than thou. Then he named a few of them who had skeletons in their closets. We bet there are quite a few yet to be discovered. Oh, dem bones!

House divided against itself (cannot stand)

Everyday conversation doesn't include many instances of this phrase, but it crops up with some regularity among pundits who are constantly assessing the inability of countries to get along internally. It comes from words of Jesus.

Mark 3:25 "And if a house be divided against itself, that house cannot stand."

Jesus' words had nothing to do with politics. He was telling his opponents why they were wrong for thinking that he cast out demons through the power of the chief of demons, Satan.

The best-known use of the phrase is President Lincoln's speech upon being nominated to be U.S. Senator from Illinois. "A house divided against itself cannot stand. I believe this government cannot endure, permanently, half slave and half free. I do not expect the Union to be dissolved—I do not expect the house to fall—but I do expect it will cease to be divided."

Simmons Research did a survey from which they collected data to attempt to understand the divide among Americans over the presidency of Donald Trump. Interestingly, they found a lot of agreement, too. "The average American probably believes in all of the values shown to characterize the two polarized groups…The great divide that seems to have split us might actually be relatively smaller than realized differences in degree, exacerbated by the heat of the election campaigns, dirty politics and media exploiting ratings potential."[86]

---

[86]Bill Harvey, "A House Divided Against Itself Cannot Stand" 17 Mar 2017 (https://www.mediavillage.com/article/a-house-divided-against-itself-cannot-stand/) 5 Jan 2019.

How are the mighty fallen

The Guardian, a London newspaper, writing a few years ago about one of England's Roman Catholic state schools, criticized it for effectively segregating students by denying entry to applicants whose parents had not served in the Catholic Church for at least three years. Said *The Guardian,* its policy was violative of the moral purpose of state education. To this school, "famously chosen by Tony Blair and Nick Clegg for their sons,"[87] the paper applied a biblical pronouncement:

2 Sam 1:25-27 "How are the mighty fallen in the midst of the battle!"

This was David's lament at the death of Jonathan, his best friend and the son of King Saul. We hardly think it applies to a school for running afoul of equal access laws. There is, in David's words, a sense of tragedy, an expression of the magnitude of the loss of potential, never to return because of death.

The saying has been used of various political, spiritual and other influential persons who have died: Abraham Lincoln; Franklin Roosevelt; John F. Kennedy; William Jennings Bryan; Martin Luther King, Jr.; and others. It has also been used of public figures who achieved prominence upon the assumption of high character and morals and then experienced a reversal of fortunes or public approbation due to their own sins. There, the fall is one of leadership, and the death is one of moral example.

And the phrase has been invoked to bemoan a shift in the position of some major religions on science: "The Catholic

---

[87]Jonathan Pierce, "Faith schools cannot continue their immoral policy of discrimination" 3 Sep 2013 (https://www.patheos.com/blogs/tippling/2013/09/03/faith-schools-cannot-continue-their-immoral-policy-of-discrimination/) 7 Jan 2019.

Church and Islam were both instrumental in the development of modern science and were the guardians of cutting-edge human knowledge in their times. How are the mighty fallen!"[88]

In a blog dedicated to "Your Life, Liberty and Happiness after the Digital Explosion," Author Harry Lewis writes about Apple Corporation's censorship of dictionaries, and much else that can be downloaded to its iPhone. In a 5 Aug 2009 entry he says Apple wouldn't allow dictionaries including entries it believed would harm the innocence of users. A comment left by a lexicographer, Nick Humez, said: "one cannot help thinking that innocence and ignorance are being conflated here, and that what Apple is doing is fostering the latter in the misguided impression that it is somehow safeguarding the former. If so, how are the mighty fallen!" In our view, Apple is certainly a mighty corporation, but we're not sure it has really fallen. We're probably just learning how low it has been all along.

---

[88] A comment by "SoMG" on "ScienceBlogs," 30 Jul 2008 (https://scienceblogs.com/pharyngula/2008/07/30/karl-giberson-strikes-back) 7 Jan 2019.

In the mire

2 Peter 2:22 "It is happened unto them according to the true proverb, The dog is turned to his own vomit again; and the sow that was washed to her wallowing in the mire."

Mire, in this verse, is simply mud. One becomes mired down in mud because it's thick and hinders movement. Someone who is in the mire is in the thick of some circumstance, complication or predicament that keeps him from making forward progress, or perhaps even from backing out. In context, Peter meant also that the mud had a destructive hold on the one who went back to it. He didn't *want* to get out.

David the Psalmist wanted to get out. He used the Hebrew version of the word in Psalm 69:2: "I sink in deep mire, where there is no standing: I am come into deep waters, where the floods overflow me." Mud or flood, he was in desperate straits.

We've seen "in the mire of materiality," "stuck in the mire of pre-modernity" (that must be really sticky), "the mire of sadness," "stymied in the mire of what might have been," and "sinking in the mire of my own stupidity." We've read, "stuck in the mire of your comfort-seeking calculations" (no doubt why the sow returned to it), "the mire of doubt" (Spurgeon), "trapped in the mire of the drug culture," "deep in the mire of folly," and "bogged down in the mire of political turmoil." "Anyone stuck in the mire of anxiety" may "often get stuck in the mire of grief"as well, but still rejoice that they have not "wallowed in the mire of their own bigotry." The more creative out there have imagined there is also "the mire of self-created vulgarity," "the mire of situational parenting," and "the mire of anthropological morals."

Who knew there were so many kinds of mud?

In the twinkling of an eye

When you saw King James or any subject of his blink, you saw the twinkling of his eye. That's all it means. Of course, in the context where it appears in Paul's letter to the Corinthian church, it takes on an implication of a very, very brief moment:

1 Corinthians 15:52 "In a moment, in the twinkling of an eye, at the last trump: for the trumpet shall sound, and the dead shall be raised incorruptible, and we shall be changed."

The idiom retains that sense today, when it is occasionally employed, which is not very often outside Christian communities, but it does happen.

For instance, Per Baekgaard, Michael Kai Petersen, and Jakob Eg Larsen write in their book about the "synchronization of EEG and eye tracking based on blink signatures," which involves "Achieving robust adaptive synchronization of multimodal biometric inputs," among other things. (These guys love the tech language.) The title of the book? *In the twinkling of an eye.* Well, of course it is.

Kingdom come

Jesus' disciples asked him how to pray. Among the few, simple requests they were to make of God, he said, were these:

Matthew 6:10 "Thy kingdom come. Thy will be done in earth, as it is in heaven."

The unifying theme of Jesus' entire ministry was the kingdom of God. This kingdom is simply the rule of God in the lives of human beings. The kingdom existed in Old Testament times, and it exists today; it simply isn't complete. The fulfillment of the kingdom comes at the end of this age when Christ returns to earth. So, "thy kingdom come" has a futuristic ring about it. In the vernacular, it simply means "the end."

Jeff Glendenning of the Kansas City Star (24 Nov 2017) says, "The Legislature could raise taxes from now to kingdom come and not keep up with demands for more spending." We feel their pain.

Eyelet Waldman commented, "I, alas, could put this chair (a Fermob chair) on every one of my holiday lists from now to Kingdom Come and never hope to find one beneath the twinkling lights of the Hanukkah menorah. But a girl can dream."

Mike Johnston, "The Online Photographer" (21 Nov 2018) wrote, "Of course, we can all argue from now to Kingdom Come about the details, from whether you should crop or not to whether B&W is realistic…"[89]

Penn Jillette (of Penn and Teller) said in an article for the Los Angeles Times, "Here in Vegas we build beautiful buildings, fill them with history, and then we blow them to kingdom come." (For instance, the Aladdin, Binion's Horseshoe, the

---

[89]https://theonlinephotographer.typepad.com/the_online_photographer/2018/11/what-it-comes-down-to-for-me.html

Dunes, Hacienda, Klondike, Lady Luck, Sahara, and the Stardust—all gone.)

A commenter on 911blog.com says, "They blew them to kingdom come right in front of the whole world." Yes, they did. And in kingdom come, they will pay.

Describing part of the movie, *Monuments Men,* a movie about men tasked to recover the art that Nazis stole during World War II, writer Lisa Pickering said, "Where churches and castles stood, German Nazis blew them to kingdom come – in some cases along with the art they held."[90]

For those who were living on another planet during 2017-2018, Robert Mueller was the special prosecutor appointed to investigate the possibility of Russian interference in the 2016 American presidential elections. Rowan Scarborough of the *Washington Examiner* wrote an explosive piece completed just before the end of 2018 which Ken Berwitz said would shortly be "blowing the Mueller 'Investigation' to kingdom come."

On Yahoo Answers, a woman asked "How do I get my husband to pick up after himself?" Answers came pouring in, almost exclusively from other women, one of whom wrote bluntly, "He isn't going to change. You could nag him from now to kingdom come and all you'll get for it is a sore throat."

---

[90]Lisa Pickering, "Monuments Men Save the Day, 12 Feb 2014 (http://guardianlv.com/2014/02/monuments-men-save-the-day/) 6 Jan 2019.

Knees knocking

Daniel 5:6 "Then the king's countenance was changed, and his thoughts troubled him, so that the joints of his loins were loosed, and his knees smote one against another."

Refer to **Writing [is] on the wall** for what so disturbed the king's countenance. Modern people still say they were so afraid or nervous their knees knocked.

NC State University advertised a Wake County spelling bee they were hosting, asking students to come out in force to support the participants. "Remember how your knees knocked as you stood in front of your whole class, trying to spell "angst" or "erudite"?[91] they said. Well, how were the little spellers going to be helped by all those college students out there spelling the words with their silent mouths as the competitors nervously called out the letters? Oh, that's right: college students can't spell.

Jason Wright, writing for FoxNews, remembers seventh grade, waiting for report cards on the last day of school in 1984. He described the scene: "His knobby knees knocked. His heart raced. His palms were so sweaty, he needed a "wet floor" sign next to his desk."[92] Wright was the young man. And he failed, by the way. So the knee knocking was justified.

Marion Flanagan describes his first experience with riding a zipline, in New Hampshire's north country. "My knees knocked together like castanets as I studied the zip cable, which looked like a giant tightrope strung over an abyss."[93] Well, yeah. Our theory is if you don't have to escape death by riding down a zipline, don't *risk* death by doing it.

---

[91](https://web.ncsu.edu/dev-news/2011/02/b-e-e-there-spellers-compete-on-campus/)
[92](https://www.foxnews.com/opinion/the-incredible-lesson-i-learned-after-i-failed-the-seventh-grade)
[93](https://www.bjtonline.com/business-jet-news/new-hampshires-north-country)

Labor of love

These days when someone says, "It was a labor of love," she's often saying more than the obvious. She's saying the person didn't get paid to do it. The source of this phrase had no such implication, but the meaning was deeply serious.

Hebrews 6:10 "For God is not unrighteous to forget your work and labour of love, which ye have shewed toward his name, in that ye have ministered to the saints, and do minister."

For Paul, "labor of love" was less something the doer *loved to do* than it was something that *showed love* to others. The contemporary phrase says more of the doer than the recipient.

The official blog of the Chicago Athletic Hotel highlights the work of one of its chefs. "Cooking, for Cindy's chef, is a true labor of love," they write. "For him, cooking comes from a deep place that he truly enjoys sharing with his team and with you, his diners." We're glad he loves his work, but we're sure he still gets paid for it. He loves that, too.[94]

An article in the *Journal of Social and Personal Relationships* said: "An actor–partner interdependence model revealed emotion work was linked to heightened future relationship satisfaction, and female partners' emotion work was the strongest predictor of both partners' relationship satisfaction."[95] Read it again if you need to; we'll wait. But the PhD. who wrote it calls "emotion work" a "labor of love."

---

[94] https://www.chicagoathletichotel.com/michigan-avenue-hotel-blog/labor-of-love
[95] Rebecca M. Horne and Matthew D. Johnson, "A Labor of Love? Emotion Work in Intimate Relationships" (https://journals.sagepub.com/doi/abs/10.1177/0265407518756779) 6 Jan 2019.

Land of the living

Anyone who has had a particularly bad case of influenza knows what it's like to be welcomed back to the land of the living—it certainly felt like they were about to be on the other side!

Psalm 27:13 "I had fainted, unless I had believed to see the goodness of the LORD in the land of the living."

Job used this same expression to ponder where wisdom might be found—he didn't believe it was to be found in the land of the living. God knows. (See: God knows.)

Today, it has the Psalmist's exact meaning. One woman described her experience after a red eye flight from Dubai to Las Vegas, leaving her feeling dead. People sometimes make the remark when someone has been away or incommunicado for a long while.

A young lady addicted to her iPad wrote that after it seemed to have crashed, she had it serviced and then welcomed it back to the land of the living. I knew iPads were important to their addicted users—and most users are, indeed, addicted—but who knew that they had a life of their own?

And in this day of fascination with zombies and their apocalypses, somebody has come up with a cocktail called the Corpse Reviver, "reputed to bring the dead back to the land of the living."[96] We wouldn't know. We've never been dead. Nor have we ever had alcoholic drinks. It's the best way never to be dead drunk.

---

[96](https://www.foxnews.com/food-drink/how-to-make-the-ultimate-zombie-cocktail) Accessed 7 Jan 2019.

Last shall be first

This useful phrase was spoken by Jesus in a warning to his Jewish hearers who thought they were shoe-ins for the kingdom of God:

Matthew 19:30 "But many that are first shall be last; and the last shall be first."

As a warning, it's useful also to anyone who touts his status as a guarantee of divine blessing.

John Dorfman advises investors, however, that it's not usually the case in his area of interest. In an article he titled "The Last Shall Be First – Or Shall They?," Dorfman leads off by saying, "'The last shall be first,' it says in the book of Matthew. How often does that happen in the stock market?" He goes on to say only about 44% of the time, based on twenty-five "disgraced" stocks that rose to beat the market index.[97]

Similarly, Charles Goren writes in *Sports Illustrated*, the Vault section, "The last shall be first—Not even seeded in the top 20, a St. Louis team survived a three-way round robin and won the Vanderbilt trophy at the Spring Nationals." In stocks or sports, the prognosticators of one's fortunes seem to be relying on the vagaries of chance rather than the providence of a just God.

---

[97]<https://www.gurufocus.com/news/791480/the-last-shall-be-first--or-shall-they> Accessed 7 Jan 2019.

Laughter is the best medicine

Reader's Digest has a column called "Laughter, the Best Medicine." It's many readers' first destination when *RD* comes in the mail. It got its name from the Bible:

Proverbs 17:22 "A merry heart doeth good like a medicine: but a broken spirit drieth the bones."

This saying has been proven true in daily life continuously and so often that it needs no scientific study to establish it. That hasn't kept scientists from studying it and trying to quantify it. It gives them a raison d'etre.

The Help Guide, an online source of friendly advice on a range of health and relationship subjects, offers this: "Laughter strengthens your immune system, boosts mood, diminishes pain, and protects you from the damaging effects of stress." They make general references to professional studies.

Psychology Today, however, weighs in on the other side. While talking about how laughter is universal and "evolved" for some purpose or other, the rag then says, "Laughter is an energetic activity that raises our heart rate and blood pressure, but these physiological effects are incompletely documented and their medicinal benefits are even less certain."[98] And on the claim that laughter and longevity are connected, *PT* says, "Does a sense of humor or a lighthearted personality add years to your life? Not necessarily." Killjoys.

It might be of interest to the reader that the article was written by Robert Provine for the November 2000 issue, which featured on its cover a picture of funny man Robin Williams. He killed himself August 11, 2014. Bummer.

---

[98]Robert Provine, "The Science of Laughter" 1 Nov 2000 <https://www.psychology today.com/us/articles/200011/the-science-laughter> Accessed 7 Jan 2019.

Law unto themselves

In December, 2018, California police officer Ronil Singh was shot dead by an illegal alien. In the next two days, a surprising network of people helped the perpetrator, Gustavo Arriaga, get away. Family members, also illegals, covered up evidence, provided transportation, money, cell phone, clothes, places to stay and whatever else he needed to escape. Cops caught him, but the event underscored what an *American Thinker* article said: "Illegals [are] a law unto themselves in California."[99]

Gangs, whether in New York, Chicago, L.A. or anywhere else, often claim boldly that they have their own system of justice. For that matter, the older organized crime families made the same boast. "We handle our own."

The saying that some people are a "law unto themselves" (or just one person, sometimes) comes from the Bible:

Rom 2:14 "For when the Gentiles, which have not the law, do by nature the things contained in the law, these, having not the law, are a law unto themselves."

Paul meant that even without the Law of God, Gentiles had enough sense of right and wrong to behave themselves, and when they disobeyed what their consciences told them, they knew they were in the wrong. Today, people have pretty much the opposite in mind: they assume the prerogative of making up their own rules and flaunting them in the face of the law of God or the laws of a country. Or as Judges 17:6 says, "In those days there was no king in Israel, but every man did that which was right in his own eyes."

---

[99]Monica Showalter, "Illegals a law unto themselves in California cop-killing case" 7 Jan 2019, https://www.americanthinker.com/blog/2019/01/illegals_a_law_unto_themselves _in_california_copkilling_case.html> Accessed 7 Jan 2019.

Led as a sheep to the slaughter

Acts 8:32 "He was led as a sheep to the slaughter"

In the most accurate use of the phrase we've found in our times, in a book by Joy Damon, she contends that "Diana's death—and the people's reaction to it—changed forever the perception and role of the British Monarchy. It did require her death. ...Princess Diana, the Lamb to the Slaughter."[100]

Australian winemaker Dave Powell has spoken out about being ousted from his own winery, Torbreck, in 2013, describing himself as "a lamb to the slaughter."[101] Well, boo hoo, but hardly a sacrifice.

The BBC reported (5 Oct 2010) that "A 62-year-old man has told a court being sexually abused by a Roman Catholic priest as a young boy left him feeling 'like a lamb to the slaughter.'" True. And reprehensible.

And the Toronto Sun ran an interview with Jane Seymour in which she finally disclosed an early experience she had long kept secret for fear of being blackballed as an actress. "Jane Seymour has accused her old agent of leading her 'like a lamb to the slaughter' by connecting her with a film maker who was known as a sexual predator during her youth."[102] We're glad Seymour made it through that tough period. If she hadn't, *Somewhere in Time* might have been very, very different. And may God wreak havoc in the lives of sexual predators.

---

[100]Joy Damon, "Princess Diana, the Lamb to the Slaughter (Bloomington, IN, iUniverse, 2002) xvi.

[101]Lucy Shaw, "Powell: I was a lamb to the slaughter" (https://www.thedrinksbusiness .com/2016/06/powell-i-was-a-lamb-to-the-slaughter/) 20 Jun 2016.

[102]https://torontosun.com/entertainment/celebrity/jane-seymour-says-agent-led-me-in-like-a -lamb-to-the-slaughter/wcm/3c4e2252-f9cd-4f76-914f-48c7619708cc, 5 Dec 2017.

Let there be light

To be accurate, the occurrence of this iconic phrase from the mouth of the Lord is almost always a play on the divine command, employed to give a biblical ring to human activities.

Genesis 1:3 "And God said, Let there be light: and there was light."

Whether it's because sayings of this kind aren't easily disguised as someone's own words or the potential metaphorical meaning would be forced, for some reason it isn't commonly heard, except in titles for inventions, programs, books and other artistic works, and of course, movies ("Let There Be Light," Viva Pictures, 2017).

There's a nonprofit organization called Let There Be Light International, which helps people in Africa get solar power. (That would change the dark continent as much as anything.)

Nature Physics lauds Arthur Ashkin and others for their work in laser physics that among other things made possible corrective eye surgery by laser. *NP* invokes the Lord's words, "Let there be light" as a plaudit. See what they did there?

A chimney sweep company sports the motto, "Let there be light" in its logo. (Chim-chiminy-chim-chim-cheree!)

Let There Be Light is the title of a documentary film about the lengthening history of the scientific quest to invent a mechanism to provide cheap, abundant energy from fusion—as opposed to fission, which is what today's nuclear power plants do. (We say more power to them.)

And the Royal Society of Chemistry published a monograph entitled: "Let there be light: stability of palmitic acid monolayers at the air/salt water interface in the presence and absence of simulated solar light and a photosensitizer." Well, that says it all.

Letter of the law

This very useful phrase crops up with regularity in the legal profession, understandably, and in church, also quite understandably. But it's widely known and used outside those contexts.

Romans 7:6 "we are delivered from the law, that being dead wherein we were held; that we should serve in newness of spirit, and not in the oldness of the letter."

Other verses, particularly from Paul's quill, mention the letter and the law in the same sentence, and they are easily put together. Jesus also said that not "one tittle of the law" would fail until all had been fulfilled. A tittle was a small mark on a Hebrew letter.

Because both Pauline passages combined "letter" with "spirit," the phrase "letter of the law" usually implies that "spirit" is somewhere in the background as the preferred alternative. The spirit of the law is the moral or ethical heart of a value that gives rise to a law that attempts to codify it.

That said, sometimes people speak of the letter of the law and mean especially to hold other people to it, with no apology made.

A woman had two dogs and walked them using electronic collars and a vibration control to keep them in check. She was ticketed for not having them on a physical leash, and she said: "This is a small matter. I will go to court. I absolutely know I violated the letter of the law. But as a political science minor, I think I learned that the Constitution makes room for people who obey the spirit of the law." Perhaps. Depends on the judge she gets.

Little bird told me

Ecclesiastes 10:20 "Curse not the king, no not in thy thought; and curse not the rich in thy bedchamber: for a bird of the air shall carry the voice, and that which hath wings shall tell the matter."

The CEV, probably echoing the prior and more conversational form of the saying, renders the last part of this verse, "A little bird might hear and tell everything." The verse is a warning against saying things you wouldn't want to get out, because they probably will.

One of the author's fond memories of his mother-in-law was her frequently explaining her inside knowledge of something by saying, "A little bird told me." She said it conspiratorially and in a helpful way.

This is an old saying and perhaps because of its altered form many people do not know its origin. Dictionaries of English idioms do not always reveal their authors' knowledge of where it came from, though they properly say it means the speaker doesn't want to reveal the source.

A columnist invited his readers to answer a question, and when readers responded via Twitter, the columnist printed the answer under the heading, "A little bird told me." Apropos.

And this passage comes from Michael Connelly, one of the author's favorite novelists, in *Void Moon* (New York, Little Brown & Company, 2002, p. 358). In a twisted confusion of events, a bad guy, Grimaldi, comes to see a partner in crime, Karch, who thinks that their target is about to appear at any time. Karch says he's a little early. But Grimaldi thinks Karch has double crossed him, and he's about to rub Karch out.

"Really?" Grimaldi interrupted. "A little bird told me she's already been here. Come and gone, as a matter of fact." (Curtains for Karch.)

Lost sheep

Like many other biblical expressions, "lost sheep" is used often in Christian circles and sometimes elsewhere. Also like many such expressions, the film, television, book and theater communities have latched onto it. It's curious how people outside the church seem fascinated with biblical phrases.

Luke 15:4 "What man of you, having an hundred sheep, if he lose one of them, doth not leave the ninety and nine in the wilderness, and go after that which is lost, until he find it?"

A UK coffee shop bears the name Lost Sheep Coffee, for reasons we haven't been able to discern. We shan't go there anytime soon, despite our love of good coffee, because according to reviewers the coffee isn't very good, it's overpriced, and the shop itself is disorganized.

A enterprise in downtown Sheboygan, WI, is called the Lost Sheep Yarn Shop. Cute.

Speaking of yarn, and not the fictitious story type, an actual sheep whose owners had reported her in 2016 as missing for six years was found where she had wandered in a forest near Tasmania, the little devil. The sheep, named Sheila, was found in a ditch beside a road, unable to move because of the weight of her soaked wool. Sheila was recovered and shorn. She had been carrying about forty-six pounds of wool. No wonder she had trouble moving around.

And finally, after Christmas one year authorities in Omaha, NE, found and took in a lost sheep. They speculated that the animal had wandered away from a live Nativity scene. Their first clue was the red and green Christmas sweater she was wearing. From the picture we saw of the garish thing, we think she wouldn't have donned the sweater herself.

Love of money is the root of all evil

Possibly the most misquoted verse in the Bible, though there would be many contenders, is from the Apostle Paul:

1 Timothy 6:10 "For the love of money is the root of all evil: which while some coveted after, they have erred from the faith, and pierced themselves through with many sorrows."

In deriving a popular saying from this verse, people often leave out "the love of" and indict money itself. Money is neither good nor bad, only useful for one or the other.

A website dedicated to open debate on random questions asked if money were truly the root of all evil. Everyone commenting said either that it was, and gave evidence, or that it wasn't, but didn't know it came from the Bible.

Another source contradicted the idea that money is the root of all evil, but it indicted ignorance instead, not covetousness.

"The *lack* of money is the root of all evil," has been attributed to Mark Twain and George Bernard Shaw. We're pretty familiar with Twain, less with Shaw, and don't feel like spending two hours to find out which is, or if both are, the source. Twain was in and out of bankruptcy, so it seems plausible he wryly said it.

Louisa May Alcott once wrote that "Money is the root of all evil, and yet it is such a useful root that we cannot get on without it any more that we can potatoes." Tubers both.

And again, the medical world references the Bible, in the case of a woman with constrictive bronchiolitis—trouble breathing. Turns out it was due either to certain gums used to make ink for printing currency, or the drugs usually found on it. Truly a case where, as they said, "money is the root of all evil"—or at least handling it was for the woman, a bank clerk.

Lukewarm

Revelation 3:16 "So then because thou art lukewarm, and neither cold nor hot, I will spue thee out of my mouth."

This widely used adjective comes from middle English and was popularized by the King James Bible. It means neither warm nor hot, as the verse in Revelation says.

Scientists who have an irresistible urge to tell us things are bad for us have been either prophets of doom or assurance. Recently they meddled more, telling us that while coffee may not cause cancer (which we never believed in the first place), if we drink any liquid above 140°, it could increase our likelihood of contracting throat cancer. They advise us to drink it lukewarm. Thanks, but no thanks. Hot but not too hot, we say.

The *Wall Street Journal* says that the hard left in America is lukewarm about Senator Elizabeth Warren as a candidate for President. She has a drop of Indian blood, it seems, but not enough to make her a brave, especially against the chief executive in office in 2019.

Why does my water heater put out lukewarm water on cold mornings, ask numerous people of the experts. The answers vary, but the reason may simply be that you need a new one.

Astrophysicists call black holes that have the same temperature as the thermal background "lukewarm." We doubt it, since they are formed from stars. Anyone sucked into one would have a hot time in star town tonight.

In early 2019 The New York Yankees were said to be lukewarm on signing Manny Machado again—why? In 2018 he batted almost 300 with 37 home runs and 107 RBIs.

And finally, some cooking site touted a summer salad they said was best served lukewarm. With greens, no less. No, no, no. Give us cool, crisp greens. Anything less gets floppy. Ugh.

Man after my own heart

Acts 13:22 " I have found David the son of Jesse, a man after mine own heart, which shall fulfil all my will."

It doesn't take much to convince some persons that another persons qualifies for this assessment. One fellow found out that a new acquaintance also liked claret and declared him "a man after my own heart." Two band members mutually declared themselves men after each other's own heart after finding out they both used subtle methods of "hijacking the audience's attention away from the singer.[103] A grandson, discovering stories and photos of his grandfather entertaining family crowds with bizarre humor, summarized his departed loved one as a man after his own heart. And a thief was inspired by the exploits of a fellow criminal and complimented him in the same way.

Nor is the compliment restricted to the male gender. Says Rev. Daren J. Zehnle, "Take 104-year-old Elizabeth Warren of Fort Worth, Texas, for example, who drinks three Dr Peppers each day (and has for almost forty years). In a recent interview, she said, "People try to give me coffee for breakfast, well, I'd rather have a Dr Pepper.' She's a woman after my own heart.'"[104]

---

[103]("Captain Sensible, in a post on https://www.facebook.com/sensiblecaptain/posts/a-man-after-my-own-heart-darkness-bassist-frankie-poullaine-and-myself-discuss-t/10157549
311248102/)

[104]On https://dzehnle.blogspot.com/2015/03/a-woman-after-my-own-heart.html,
posted 20 Mar 2015, Accessed 8 Jan 2019.

Man does not live by bread alone

Often shortened to "not by bread alone," this expression came out of the experience of Jesus in the wilderness being tempted by Satan to compromise his mission on earth before it really got started.

Matthew 4:4 "It is written, Man shall not live by bread alone, but by every word that proceedeth out of the mouth of God."

Sometimes writers acknowledge the truth of the saying but go on to make their point that if bread is in short supply, it becomes pretty important, whatever else humanity needs. Andrei Kolesnikov wrote about Russian hunger in *Gazeta:* "Wherever Russians eat, they always look for the bread on the table. Russia has a cultural stereotype of bread as something of great value and the stuff of life. Yet, in reality, the cult of bread—and the Russian superstition against wasting it or throwing it out—is a historical consequence of decades of hunger."[105]

Martha Stewart appears to take issue with the negative form of the expression, in "By Bread Alone: Making Dough" *(https://www.marthastewart.com/274268/by-bread-alone-making-dough-0)* an article devoted to the homemaker who wants bread on her (or his) table every time.

And the Jewish site OUKosher.com agrees that life should not be lived by bread alone: you also need potatoes. As the writer put it, "A potato is, as Rabbi Miller put it, 'like a whole bagel coming right out of the ground!'"

---

[105] Andrei Kolesnikov, "By Bread Alone: Why Poor Russians Aren't Protesting" (https://carnegie.ru/commentary/62491) Accessed 9 Jan 2019.

Manna from heaven

When the Hebrews exited Egypt they quickly found themselves in the Sinai desert with nothing to eat. God's provision was manna.

Psalm 78:24 "And had rained down manna upon them to eat, and had given them of the corn of heaven."

"Corn" in this verse refers to grain, specifically wheat; the word has changed in the past 400 years. "Manna," as most other versions translate it, is rightly rendered, "What is it?" That's the literal meaning of the word. In colloquial English today we would say, "whatsit," or "whatchamacallit." The Hebrews had no idea what it was, and the term, "what is it" stuck. It was like bread and it came down from heaven in the night.

Jesus later commented on the miraculous provision, when he described himself as the true bread from heaven, in John 6:31: "Our fathers did eat manna in the desert; as it is written, He gave them bread from heaven to eat."

Predictably, restaurants like to call themselves by something with "manna" in the name. So do church ministries feeding the hungry. There's even a brewery in New York with "Manna" in its moniker. We suppose that when it snows there, while some people are raiding the stores for bread and milk, Manna Brewery recommends milk and beer. Well, it *is* made from barley and yeast.

Men of the world

Alfred P. Doolittle famously negotiated with Professor Higgins in George Bernard Shaw's *Pygmalion* (and the musical, *My Fair Lady*), for the return of his daughter, Eliza, or else a price for her.

DOOLITTLE. Listen here, Governor. You and me is men of the world, ain't we?
HIGGINS. Oh! Men of the world, are we? You'd better go, Mrs. Pearce.
MRS. PEARCE. I think so, indeed, sir.

The idea of "men of the world" has, attached to it, a sense of, shall we say, refined vulgarity. Men of the world are presumed to be anything but innocent of the pleasures of sophisticated life, including its indulgences. At the very least, they are not shocked by the immorality they encounter.

The expression comes from the Psalms, and its implications have not much changed.

Psalm 17:14 "From men which are thy hand, O LORD, from men of the world, which have their portion in this life, and whose belly thou fillest with thy hid treasure: they are full of children, and leave the rest of their substance to their babes."

In 2010, Radox, best known for their bubble bath and shower gels, launched a new product, Radox Men, an all-in-one shower gel and shampoo. Its marketing slogan was, "designed for men of the world." They probably put it right next to their exfoliating shower puffs. Whatever happened to *soap?* And *men*, for that matter?

Milk and honey

Also the fuller, "flowing with milk and honey," this expression refers to a place or condition with abundant provisions. It's found in several Bible verses, including this one:

Deuteronomy 26:9 "And he hath brought us into this place, and hath given us this land, even a land that floweth with milk and honey.

Not many people use the phrase in daily conversation, but it shows up in the names of: lip balm; a color of sandals; fragrance oil; smoothie drinks; hand lotion; a women's day festival; a play by John Lennon and Yoko Ono; a T-shirt; a book (actually several of them); a photography studio; dinner rolls; body wash; a paint color; a beer; a hand soap; and stretch mark butter. And the list goes on. But not here.

Millstone around one's neck

The image that always comes to the author's mind is the millstone he saw in Israel a few years ago, fully three feet in diameter and ten or more inches thick. We assume, just from a logistical standpoint, that the one spoken of in the following verse was quite a bit smaller, but sufficiently heavy for the purpose.

Luke 17:2 "It were better for him that a millstone were hanged about his neck, and he cast into the sea, than that he should offend one of these little ones."

With this metaphor Jesus was trying to make a very, very serious point about the damage people do to the most innocent among us, our children. Whether through influence (which was his specific point) or abuse, which would also qualify, people who sully and spoil the potential of children to know and love God are worthy of the most terrible judgment.

At a parliamentary debate in New Zealand in 1950 the discussion was whether to adopt a capital punishment bill. A Mr. Roberts, who opposed the bill, said he would gladly shoot anyone he saw committing a vile crime on a woman or child, but he wouldn't put a rope around his neck and kill him. His debate opponent countered:

The Hon. Dr. Mazengarb: Would the honorable member put a millstone around his neck and drown him?

The Hon. Mr. Roberts: No, by the time I had the millstone I would have forgiven him.

The Hon. Dr. Mazengarb: The Carpenter said something about that.

The Hon. Mr. Roberts: Yes, and the Carpenter suffered at the hands of the people that thought that capital punishment and murder were right.

Dr. Mazengarb was implying that Jesus (the Carpenter) recommended capital punishment in our verse above. We don't read it that way. He was, however, acknowledging that people were put to death that way sometimes.

A news outlet reporting the exciting (we exaggerate) events going on in the world of cricket said that player Virat Kohli didn't do very well when he came to England to play. The trouble was his series average of 13.40 — not very good. "If not quite a millstone round his neck it was at least a particularly persistent insect that insisted on flying near his head."[106] Doesn't quite measure up to the seriousness of capital punishment.

Educator John Carroll used the metaphor in its original sense: "In so far as the intention of education is to train the child for a vocation it is a millstone around his neck."[107] We wonder what his animus toward school is?

Anna Quindlen, rather famous writer for the *New York Times,* expressed her disapprobation toward then President George H. W. Bush over the Gulf War he was then prosecuting. In a Thanksgiving weekend article she said, "Vietnam hangs like Marley's ghost over these holiday celebrations, ready to provide us with the present and future contained in the past. For the President, this is as much a millstone around his neck as all the chains and cash boxes were around Marley's." We think history has vindicated Bush.

---

[106]Charles Reynolds, "India vs England..." 3 Aug 2018 (https://www.news18.com/cricketnext/news/reynolds-virat-kohli-swats-aside-millstone-aro und-his-neck-with-imperious-performance-1832289.html) Accessed 9 Jan 2019.

[107]John Carroll, Break-Out from the Crystal Palace (London, Routledge Publishing Co. 1974) 34.

Mind your own business

One casual etymologist opines that most theologians don't think this expression comes from the Bible. He didn't say which theologians he polled, and we doubt that if he did, he polled many. We think the expression comes from the Bible. Like some other sayings, the form has changed a bit to keep up with the times language-wise.

1 Thessalonians 4:11 "And that ye study to be quiet, and to do your own business, and to work with your own hands, as we commanded you."

The Greek behind the key words is *prassein ta idia,* which is rough in English—attend to the own. "Your" is understood, and "own," since it's an adjective, implies a noun, which would be gathered from the context—"stuff," "things," or "business," or any relatively vague reference to what is "your own." The KJV's rendering is good, but "mind your own business" is up to date and has been for a while.

This is such a pervasively used expression as to need no illustration to help anyone understand it. But here's one example anyway, from a forum known to take everyday speech and wryly give it a new turn of phrase:

Why don't you mind your own business?
Mind your own business
'Cause if you mind your business, then you won't be mindin' mine. —Hank Williams, *Mind Your Own Business.*

Moment of time

When we're trying to express how something took place all at once, and yet perhaps many things were compressed into that instant, we might say they took place in a moment in time.

Luke 4:5 "And the devil, taking him up into an high mountain, shewed unto him all the kingdoms of the world in a moment of time."

Luke's use of the expression "moment of time" is precisely equivalent to "moment *in* time," and it is because of the expression that we are able to interpret this part of Jesus' temptation experience as occurring in his mind, through a vivid, waking dream, or what we would call a vision. The account gives us a sense of the mystery or wonder of what can seem to take hours and/or involve distant travel and yet happen in an instant.

A Moment in Time Bridal Shop seems especially apropos. The happily and lengthily married have a book of memories of that day, the hour, and the moment they said, "I do." In a way, it's frozen in time.

Our favorite use of the phrase is in a hauntingly lovely tune by Beth Nielsen Chapman, with the phrase as the title:

One moment in time,
And I knew why I had waited so long;
One look in your eyes
Meant forever from that moment on.[108]

---

[108]Songwriters: Steve Dorff / Beth Nielsen Chapman, "The Moment You Were Mine" lyrics © Warner/Chappell Music, Inc

My cup runneth over

Psalm 23:5 "Thou preparest a table before me in the presence of mine enemies: thou anointest my head with oil; my cup runneth over."

In *It's a Wonderful Life,* George Bailey's brother, Harry, has come home from college with two new things in his life. One is Mrs. Harry Bailey, and the other is a position in his wife's company. George's Uncle Billy declares, "Oh, he gets you *and* a job? Harry's cup runneth over!"[109]

A journal soberly warns those prone to drinking too much during the holidays that there are hazards when your cup runneth over a little too much.

Ed Ames (et al.) memorably recorded, "My Cup Runneth Over with Love."

Cuprunnethover.com is a coffee company. We don't know about the readers, but when a coffee cup runs over hands often get burned. The wrong image is conjured up, we say.

DACBeachcroft wrote that in planning for the 2018 Soccer World Cup match, "The cup runneth over for insurers."[110] The premiums, it seems, were not far from what it would have cost to pay the claims, for such things as cancellation insurance, terrorism insurance, etc. Some people got a lot of money for doing next to nothing. Because nothing bad happened. (France beat Croatia 4-2.)

---

[109]Frank Capra, *It's a Wonderful Life* (RKO Radio Pictures, Inc. 1946)

[110](https://www.dacbeachcroft.com/en/gb/articles/2018/july/insuring-the-world-cup-the-cup-runneth-over-for-insurers/) Accessed 9 Jan 2019.

No rest for the wicked

Matt Shultz of the band Cage the Elephant said a hit song was "inspired by an old co-worker of his who at the time was a drug dealer. When Shultz asked him why he dealt drugs, the co-worker told him, 'There's no rest for the wicked.'"

Isaiah 57:20 "But the wicked are like the troubled sea, when it cannot rest, whose waters cast up mire and dirt."

Isaiah was being as serious as a heart attack when he wrote those words. The expression based on this verse, however, is usually spoken with some level of sarcasm or jesting.

History.com advertised the continuation of its hit series Vikings: "There is no rest for the wicked. Vikings will descend deeper into madness tonight on History." Those are indeed some wicked looking dudes.

The Sun said that "December was a fantasy football frenzy. We had games coming out of our ears across the festive period... but there's no rest for the wicked in January."[111]

Roya Backlund writes on *Elite Daily*, "Your laptop is definitely with you at all times so that you can reply to work emails and keep your goals on track. There's no rest for the wicked."[112] Wonder why she thinks you're wicked?

And on Twitter, someone calling himself Satan says succinctly, "Whoever said 'there's no rest for the wicked' was lying; we love sleep." To my knowledge, Satan never sleeps.

---

[111](https://www.thesun.co.uk/dream-team/fantasy-football/8147612/ fantasy-football-tips-best-premier-league-players-January/) Accessed 9 Jan 2019

[112]https://www.elitedaily.com/p/the-1-thing-you-cant-leave-behind- when-traveling-according-to-your-zodiac-sign-15726666 Accessed 9 Jan 2019

No man can serve two masters

This expression is found in two places in the gospels, one in Matthew, the other in Luke. Matthew's version is closer to the contemporary recollection, and Luke's gives the specific context of it when it was said (which may have been more than once).

Matthew 6:24 "No man can serve two masters: for either he will hate the one, and love the other; or else he will hold to the one, and despise the other. Ye cannot serve God and mammon.

Luke's context shows Jesus was talking about stewardship—the management for God's purposes of everything he has lent us to handle. Mammon is money. They are conflicting deities.

The expression has been applied broadly, whenever a pundit sees a conflict in a public figure, for instance—whether it really exists or not.

We remember vividly when John F. Kennedy was campaigning for election to be President. In some circles around the country there was concern that Kennedy, a Roman Catholic, would be ruled by the Church: could he serve two masters—the people who elected him and the Pope, too?

It was mostly anti-Catholic sentiment that charged that argument, we think, but the question has been asked since about others with strong religious commitments. Most recently it was Mitt Romney, famously a Mormon. Tricia Erickson's 2011 book, *Can Mitt Romney Serve Two Masters?: The Mormon Church versus the Office of The Presidency of The United States of America,* (WestBow Press, Bloomington, IN) expressed alarm in most vehement terms about the prospect of Romney's election.

Nuno F. da Cruz and Rui Cunha Marques coauthored *Mixed companies and local governance: no man can serve two masters,* an article about the difficulty, if not impossibility, of water, waste, transportation, and education services operating successfully under both public and private control at the same time. In this country, one thinks of certain "faith based initiatives" of government that have proposed some services be handled by churches (etc.) and paid for by government. Since when did anyone *ever* know of an organization that took government money and wasn't eventually controlled by the government?

In this country, The National Academy of Sciences conducted a study in 1974 for the EPA during which it was watched closely by two, essentially competing, congressional committees: the House Appropriations Subcommittee on Agricultural-Environmental and Consumer Protection (whew!) and the Senate Environmental Pollution Subcommittee. The former was critical of the EPA and the latter supportive of it. *Science* magazine at the time opined that the Academy wouldn't be able to serve two masters. We think the Senate had the upper hand, for a while, anyway.

And finally, Chih-Wei Hsieh, a professor at the City University of Hong Kong, says in his article, "No man can serve two masters..." that "Love of money (LOM) signifies self-interest. At first glance, it is incompatible with the altruistic notion of public service motivation (PSM). A recent study based in China, however, indicated that LOM can interact with PSM to enhance job satisfaction." Uh, Mr. Hsieh, we think you'll find that in the dictionary under "enlightened self-interest." It ain't nothin' new.

No room in the inn

A Christmas program at a Boone County, WV, elementary school was cancelled in 2018 because of *one* parent's complaint about religious content. In response, the people in the program set up their nativity scene on the side of the road and held forth. Said one newscaster, "When there's no room in the inn, you have to compromise."[113] We think she meant "improvise." "No room at the inn" comes from the birth narrative of Jesus in the gospel of Luke.

Luke 2:7 "And she brought forth her firstborn son, and wrapped him in swaddling clothes, and laid him in a manger; because there was no room for them in the inn."

First, our usual reminder: there's no innkeeper in the text. Therefore we can't draw any lesson from scripture that has anything to do with one. Next, we note that the contemporary use of the expression is sometimes literal but often metaphoric.

Among the literal usage would be the school that made no room for a nativity scene. Also literal is the Reuters report titled, "No room in the inn: central Europe student housing crunch attracts investors." It described a Polish college student opting to stay in a private home rather than in an old dormitory. Said the student, "The other dorms were really old from the communist times and really simple; I couldn't be comfortable sharing a room and a bathroom with four people."[114] We say, "Waaa!" The author spent his first two years in college in dormitories, sharing a room with two and a bathroom with eight. Most students we knew did.

---

[113]WOWK Television, 20 Dec 2018 (https://www.wowktv.com/news/no-room-in-the-inn-_20181221001134/1669626644) Accessed 10 Jan 2019.
[114](https://www.thehindu.com/news/international/no-room-in-the-inn-central-europe-student-housing-crunch-attracts-investors/article25274312.ece) Accessed 10, Jan 2019.

The metaphoric use of the expression is usually rife with political bias and not a small amount of inaccuracy. *The St. Louis Post Dispatch* published a letter about the 2018-2019 debate and dispute in the federal government about how to address the crisis at the southern border of the U.S. The writer expressed his complete enmity with President Trump:

We have just finished celebrating the birth of a baby boy who was born in a stable because the innkeeper said there was no room in the inn. In a symbolic way, the "national innkeeper" has decided that there is no room in our inn for "invaders, criminals, carriers of disease, terrorists and dirty people" so he has chased them away adding a couple of new wrinkles: He has torn little children away from their parents, and, to add insult to injury, they were gassed. So much for a so-called Christian nation.[115]

There's much wrong with this opinion, starting with the misrepresentation of the administration's actions, the failure to report the attacks of the migrant caravan on border patrol, and the fact that the policy of separating children from "parents" (which they frequently were not) predates Trump. But what really irks us is the application of Luke 2:7 to the whole situation. It's entirely invalid. It has nothing to do with illegal immigration. Mary and Joseph weren't immigrants or homeless people, and—did we say it?—there *was no innkeeper.* And anyway, exactly what problem does the writer have with keeping criminals and terrorists out of our country?

---

[115] Arthur Robles, in a letter to the editor, *St. Louis Post Dispatch* (https://www.stltoday.com/opinion/mailbag/no-room-in-the-inn-for-immigrants/article_ed2c8eac-86df-5446-80ca-c42d78e7de2b.html) Accessed 10 Jan 2019.

Nothing new under the sun

The global warming a/k/a climate change movement says that man causes the earth's temperature to rise. That's not new. But whereas some focus on the Industrial Revolution as the time when man started destroying the earth, others don't let humanity off so easy. As far back as 2009 *The Economist* ran a story in which the editors chimed, "Nothing new under the sun," and then opined, "Anthropogenic global warming started when people began farming." Well, that doesn't leave us anywhere to go, does it? It doesn't matter how much technology we would have to scrap or how much progress we would have to repent of: we would still be at fault for global warming, if you accept this argument.

The expression "nothing new under the sun" comes from the Old Testament:

Ecclesiastes 1:9 - The thing that hath been, it is that which shall be; and that which is done is that which shall be done: and there is no new thing under the sun.

It should be said that Solomon was not handing down a universal truth with absolutely no exceptions. He was observing a general truth with astounding accuracy. This is what's usually meant by a "proverb."

Inventors and developers frequently run into the proverbial truth. An inventor of a new musical instrument went to have it patented only to find out that someone had already patented something almost just like it. Car makers tout the innovation of electric and hybrid cars—hoping, we suppose, that people have not read their history books, which tell us of the first electric cars in 1897 and the first hybrids in 1917.

Nothing but skin and bones

Many a man or woman past forty can remember having been told such a thing by his or her worried mother who didn't think the child had been eating right, off at school or such. Ah, for those days.

The saying comes from the Old Testament, where Job laments the ravages of his physical ailments.

Job 19:19-20 "All my intimate friends detest me; those I love have turned against me. I am nothing but skin and bones."

Job was emaciated, as from malnutrition. In his case, it was apparently disease.

Almost never do we hear the expression as a compliment, except perhaps by those enamored of runway models, who typically are required to be sticks with faces. For normal society, a bit more flesh is required.

We often hear the expression in reference to animals. A girl wrote how she found a dog at her door who had (she knew, because she knew whom he belonged to) left his abusive owners and sought a new human to attach himself to. "He was all skin and bones," she said, "and I finally just took him in. They didn't deserve him."

And for the motorcyclist who made good in 2016 on his dream of making a long trip to Sturgis, SD, for the annual rally, the Motorcycles as Art exhibit at the Buffalo Chip featured a display curated by Michael Lichter. It was called the "Skin & Bones Exhibition," and it consisted of "Tattoo-Inspired Motorcycles and Art." It was just what it sounds like. We think we'll keep our motorcycle where it belongs.

O ye of little faith

This is one of those expressions found often in the religious community but also outside it among those who are familiar with Jesus' mild rebuke.

Matthew 14:31 "O thou of little faith, wherefore didst thou doubt?

The expression seems to crop up a lot in comments about sports, where people lose confidence in underdogs. Todd Johnson wrote about those lovable losers from the Windy City: "O, ye of little faith: Cubs tie up NLDS and take away home field advantage."[116] They didn't win it that year, but they did the next, for the first time in 108 years. Why didst thou doubt?

BYUtiful wrote on the CougarBoard (www.cougerboard .com), in reference to QB Zack Wilson, "O ye of little faith; Did it occur to you that ZW might just never fail to get a completion next season?" But he did.

Sports writer Steve Dilbeck championed the cause of the L.A. Dodgers in 2001 with this encouragement: "O ye of little faith: Mattingly says these Dodgers have chance to make playoffs."[117] They didn't. Faith doesn't make up for losing.

TV show "Jeopardy" featured the category, "O ye of little faith," with a question—excuse us, an *answer*—"Atheists disavow the existence of a god; these people from the Greek for unknowable say they aren't sure." The correct *question* was, "What is an agnostic." The answer *should* be, "somebody who had better make up his mind before he keels over."

---

[116]Todd Johnson, 10 Oct 2015 (https://cubscentral.wordpress.com/2015/10/10/o-yee-of-little-faith-cubs-tie-up-nlds-and-take-away-home-field-advantage/) Accessed 11 Jan 2019.
[117]Steve Dilbeck, 15 May 2011 (https://latimesblogs.latimes.com/dodgers/2011/05/o-ye-of-little-faith-mattingly-says-these-dodgers-have-chance-to-make-playoffs.html) Accessed 11 Jan 2019.

Oh my God

It is highly arguable, of course, that an appeal to God, or in this case an interjection containing his name, could come from any religion. We argue that it comes from the Judeo-Christian texts, and it's no compliment that it does. Today's use of the expression is almost always as a surprised utterance that takes the Lord's name in vain, which the Bible forbids.

Ezra 9:6 "O my God, I am ashamed and blush to lift up my face to thee, my God: for our iniquities are increased over our head, and our trespass is grown up unto the heavens."

This expression is truly ubiquitous. On the lips of 99% of the population it seems, it is uttered as easily as, "Oh!" and without thought to its sense. We can remember when we would have tasted soap if we had said it in childhood. Ezra, Nehemiah, Daniel, the Psalmist and others said it in the Bible fully meaning to address the Lord. Today it is an interjection said by people who have no intention of inviting God to look their way (which, of course, he is already doing, and we don't think he likes it). It should be spelled "Oh," however, considering its specific meaning in most contexts.

We'll give just one example among billions spoken daily around the globe. A resident in Vieques, Puerto Rico described what it was like when Hurricane Maria roared through: "Oh, my God, the earth shook!"[118] Yes, and it will again. Count on it. And stop saying that.

---

[118]Anonymous, on Weather.com, 27 Sep 2017 (https://weather.com/storms/hurricane/video/oh-my-god-the-earth-shook) Accessed 11 Jan 2019.

Old as the hills

Nowadays I hear, "older than dirt," about as often, but people still say things are as old as the hills.

Job 15:7 "Art thou the first man that was born? or wast thou made before the hills?"

The CEV renders the verse, "Were you the first human? Are you older than the hills? Depending on the theory of origins to which you subscribe, the hills are pretty old.

Speaking of the royal tombs of Thebes, author Harris Cowper wrote that "they are not actually as old as the hills, but they are the oldest monuments of Egypt and of the world."[119]

Chocolate is found to be as "old as the hills...[it] has now been found to be a 10 million-year-old treat. Research led by the Royal Botanic Garden Edinburgh (RBGE) suggests that cacao trees evolved about 10 million years ago."[120] It doesn't last that long in my house.

Writes a reader of Tucson.com, "As a responsible guardian of planet earth who also happens to be as old as the hills, I have tried to address the environmental and social causes championed on the covers of Time Magazine. Their articles have proclaimed, 'by the year 2000 [terrible thing] will happen'...Now I'm supposed to be diligently working climate change, previously global warming, previously weather. There's always a new cause before we fix the last one. I'm still working acid rain."[121] Ain't it the truth.

---

[119]Harris Cowper, *The Journal of Sacred Literature and Biblical Record, Volume 8,* (Whitefish, MT, Kessinger Publishing, 1859) 235.

[120]George Mair, "Chocolate is found to be as old as the hills," (*The Times, UK,* 10 Nov 2015)

[121]Jeffrey McConnell, in "Letters" 4 Dec 2018 (https://tucson.com/opinion/letters/politics-national/ etter-old-as-the-hills-and-remember-everything/article_d8079216-f7ef-11e8-b9e4-af5777f51c2d.html) Accessed 11 Jan 2019.

Out of the mouth of babes

Matthew 21:16 "And Jesus saith unto them, Yea; have ye never read, Out of the mouth of babes and sucklings thou hast perfected praise?"

Jesus called to his hearers' attention the fact that children are usually lacking in the hypocrisy, pride, pretense and other things that inhibit praise and pure enjoyment of the Lord. And what they say sometimes startles with its candor and perception.

Like many memorable biblical phrases this one gets put in titles of book, magazine articles, and scientific studies:

"Out of the Mouth of Babes: Earliest Stages in Language Learning."

"Out of the mouth of babes and sucklings: Breastfeeding and weaning in the past."

"Out of the mouth of babes: 6-11 year-olds reflect on learning Black historical narratives." A study from Hannah More Primary School in Bristol, UK.

"Out Of The Mouth's Of Babes: 14-Year-Old Pens Deep Poem." The poem is very negative if read from top to bottom. But read bottom to top, it's optimistic. Not bad for a young teen. We know somebody who wrote a love poem in which the first letters spelled out the name of his (future) wife. He will remain anonymous.

"Out of the Mouth of Babes: Children's Lemonade Money Going to Hospital." They set up a stand outside their home and waved posters at people driving by. A little pricey at $2.00. They made/donated $58.00. If they'd lowered the price to a dollar they probably could have gotten three or four times that.

"Out of the Mouth of Babes: 11-Year-Old Kid Calls Dallas City Council Members Out for Being Rude to Constituents." You go, guy!

Ox in a ditch

The author's pastor-father was fond of saying he presumed someone who was absent from church must have an ox in a ditch. The saying comes from a teaching of Jesus.

Luke 14:5 "Which of you shall have an ass or an ox fallen into a pit, and will not straightway pull him out on the sabbath day?"

Jesus called the Pharisees on their hypocrisy. They were outraged that he healed people on the Sabbath (Saturday). In addition to the law of Moses they had reams (well, scrolls) full of additional laws that purported to be applications of the 4th Commandment against work on the Sabbath. Jesus showed them by their own conduct that when it's necessary to preserve life and health, the fact that it's the Sabbath is not prohibitive.

Apparently most people have gotten the message. Writes Rina Marie, "Although today was [the] Sabbath, Jon and I spent most of the day putting up a new shelter for the goats, thanks to my crummy organizational skills."[122] It wasn't the Sabbath, we discovered, but Sunday. Some Christians just call it the Sabbath, to the consternation of their Jewish friends.

An old story is told about men in church getting up during the prayer and leaving the service. "A wildcat was in the ravine...The wildcat was soon dispatched; those men would neither leave an ox in a ditch or a wildcat in the ravine on the Sabbath day."[123]

A printing company specializing in product labels advertises, "We don't solicit same day service, but under the right circumstances it is available to loyal customers who

---

[122]Rina Marie, "Ox in a ditch," 9 Aug 2015 (http://blog.rinamarie.com/2015/08/09/ox-in-a-ditch/) Accessed 12 Jan 2019.
[123]Faye Hempstead, *Historical Review of Arkansas: Its Commerce, Industry and Modern Affairs, Volume 1* (Chicago, Lewis Publishing Co. 1911) 565.

might find their 'ox in a ditch.'" Wonder how $loyal$ you have to be?

But there's confusion in some minds about the meaning of the proverbial ox. Sports writer Don Williams wrote about a Texas Tech match up with Baylor in 2016. He said, "When the Red Raiders lost a game under Spike Dykes, it was usually because they were either A) hit by a rollin' ball o' butcher knives, B) got their ox in a ditch or C) combination of both. Either way, it made for a Bad Day at Black Rock." We're not sure what he meant by "ox in a ditch" in this context. Maybe Coach Dykes wasn't, either.

Unfortunately, some people who ought to understand the allusion to the ox don't. Actor-Senator Fred Thompson is an example. "In 2001, New York Times columnist William Safire wrote Thompson to ask what he had meant when he said 'the ox is in the ditch' when it comes to postal reform. 'Once again, you remind me that the rest of the country doesn't necessarily use the same phrases as a country boy from Tennessee,' Thompson replied, confessing he'd actually never seen an ox in a ditch—or frankly, an ox." Thompson said: "As usual, I have no idea where this comes from."[124] Fred was reared in the Church of Christ. Shame on you, Fred. Well, he's beyond that, now. Fred died in 2015.

But Fred was closer than Park Jie-won, the People's Party floor leader in South Korea in July of 2016. "South Korea is an ox in a ditch. We need to eat the grass of the U.S., but we also have to feed on the grass of China."[125] They must have their own idiom over there. Different ox, different problem.

---

[124]Holly Bailey, "Hundreds of Boxes…" (Newsweek, 19 June 2007)
[125]In the *Korea Herald,* 11 Jul 2016 (http://www.koreaherald.com/common_ prog/newsprint.php?ud=20160711000631&dt=2) Accessed 12 Jan 2019.

Patience of Job

This widely used expression comes from the Letter of James in the New Testament.

James 5:11 "…Ye have heard of the patience of Job, and have seen the end of the Lord; that the Lord is very pitiful, and of tender mercy."

By "patience," James meant the epochal variety. Nevertheless, Job's example is invoked for many mundane circumstances.

"The staff has the patience of Job," says someone leaving a comment about the Old Armory Steak House in Camden, SC. The question is, do their customers need patience, too?

Bob Chapman builds clocks. "Building a clock movement 'takes a different person,' he says. 'It takes the patience of Job' and a wide array of tools, some of which must be handmade."[126] We concur. The author took apart and reassembled a clock movement once. He had a time figuring out what made it tick.

Then there's Scott Smith, of the *Greensboro News & Record*, (NC) who, given an assignment to write on "cliches," wrote an 801 word column with 107 cliches in it. Well, actually they weren't all cliches, which means overused or lacking in original thought. However, all of them were expressions, idioms, sayings—kind of like the ones in this book—including this passage: "Let's face it, it would take the patience of Job to write the book on cliches—you know, the whole shootin' match."[127] We know, Scott. But time flies when you're having fun.

---

[126]Amy McRary, "Collectors all wound up over insides of clocks" (Deseret News, 12 Aug 2001) (https://www.deseretnews.com/article/858132/Collectors-all- wound-up-over-insides-of-clocks.html) Accessed 12 Jan 2019.
    [127]Scott Smith, "Write about cliches? It's easier said than done" (Greensboro News & Record, 15 April 1999)

Peace offering

Adherents to religions around the world claim "peace offering" comes from their sacred scriptures. However, the English language was the product of localized influences in the British Isles and borrowed influences from surrounding European lands, and the greatest religious element in that influence was Christianity. It's safe to say that the etymology of "peace offering" would trace it back to the Old Testament.

Leviticus 3:1 "And if his oblation be a sacrifice of peace offering, if he offer it of the herd; whether it be a male or female, he shall offer it without blemish before the LORD

This and other verses in the Old Testament describe the offering the Jews were to make to invoke peace between them and the Lord by atoning for their sin.

Today, anytime someone brings some sort of gift or does a favor for a person he or she has wronged, it's likely to be called a peace offering. And some strange things are offered.

In "Six tips to make up with your SO [significant other] after a fight," author Shraddha Kamdar suggests "Take him a peace offering if you have to, it could be a card, a silly soft toy or even a pair of sexy underwear." For a guy?[128] Maybe that's the ticket in India, where the writer is based.

A blogger on LiveJournal called Hauntings told of going to Graceland, Elvis's home in Memphis, TN. She thought she might have offended him (his ghost) by trying to take pictures of his Cadillac. All her digital pictures from the trip were corrupted. Someone commented, "I guess if you go back you

---

[128]Shraddha Kamdar, Six tips to make up with your SO after a fight" (*Femina*, 2 Aug 2018) (https://www.femina.in/relationships/love-sex/tips-to-make-up-with-your-partner-after-a-fight-100109-1.html)

should take him a peace offering consisting of a Fried Peanut Butter and Jelly Sandwich."[129]

The Sooke News Mirror in British Columbia printed an article about peacemaking between tribes there, some 150 years ago. Ida Jones, wife of Chief Queesto of the Pacheedaht people of Port Renfrew, gave this account: "There was a war between Indians of different tribes. A long time ago, Kitty's father, the chief, he wanted to stop the war. He wanted to save the people of his village. So he gave his daughter away. A very young girl, maybe 13 or 14, he held her up and showed her, a peace offering, to stop the war."[130] Who giveth this women to..."

Joseph Hall, working with the National Park Service in 1937, was devoted to documenting Appalachian cultural ways. He used the job to gather tidbits while working in the Great Smoky Mountains National Park in North Carolina. He went to see a Mrs. Enloe, who fished with live bait where the Park didn't allow it. She told him, "I fish when I please, winter or summer. See that can of worms?" But Hall was prepared to appease her. He said, "She showered me with praise when I gave her a peace offering, a box of snuff, and [she] let me take her picture." The author has known some of those mountain folks. If they dip, snuff's the stuff that will buy good will.

And finally, in 2012 Israel held out an olive branch. Sort of. "In a strange peace offering, on Thursday Israel transferred the bodies of 91 terrorists to the Palestinian Authority and Gaza. They had been interred in an enemy combatants' cemetery in the Jordan Valley."[131] Not quite a dozen roses or a box of candy, was it. Whatever works.

---

[129](https://hauntings.livejournal.com/576806.html) Accessed 12 Jan 2019.

[130]Elida Peers, "Owechemis: was a Nitinat Princess" in the *Sooke News Mirror, 9 Oct 2013* (https://www.sookenewsmirror.com/community/owechemis-was-a-nitinat-princess/)

[131]P. David Hornik, "Terrorist Corpses for Peace?" (http://frontpagemag.com/2012/06/01/terrorist-corpses-for-peace/) Accessed 12 Jan 2019.

Physician heal thyself

Some writers refer the reader of this proverb to the Latin, *medice cura te ipsum*, which in English is, "Physician, cure yourself." The expression appears in some Greek texts as early as the sixth century B.C., principally from Aeschylus, Greek poet and tragedian (525 B.C. – 456 B.C.).

There was no English language then, of course. And when the King James Version of the Bible was translated, the words of Aeschylus were not a well known proverb. Once the Great Bible and then the KJV went into print, however, the proverb took hold, precisely because Jesus used it the way he did.

Luke 4:23 "And he said unto them, Ye will surely say unto me this proverb, Physician, heal thyself: whatsoever we have heard done in Capernaum, do also here in thy country."

Jesus wasn't addressing doctors to give them advice to treat themselves when they are sick. He was putting words in the mouths of people in the synagogue in Nazareth, who were whispering about how they knew him growing up there. They were looking askance at him after his recitation from Isaiah and his identification of himself as the one about whom Isaiah prophesied. He rightly adjudged that they wouldn't accept him because they believed they knew all there was to know about him.

Writes Richard Lehman, "The townsfolk of Nazareth, recognizing him as the son of Joseph the carpenter, ...chase him out of town—so proving his point that it is faith which accomplishes miracles, and that you can't have faith in somebody you knew in short trousers."[132]

---

[132]Richard Lehman, 8 Jan 2007 (https://blogs.bmj.com/bmj/2007/01/08/ proverb-of-the-week-physician-heal-thyself/) Accessed 13 Jan 2019.

Christopher Carosa took the expression more in the sense of an indictment of hypocrisy: "How do you expect anyone to follow your financial or retirement planning advice if you don't follow it yourself?"[133]

For the same reason, in 2016 Sen. Chuck Grassley (R) Iowa, chided Chief Justice John Roberts of the U.S. Supreme Court. Roberts had lamented the politicization of the confirmation process for SCOTUS nominees. Grassley said, "The Justices themselves have gotten political...too often there is little difference between the actions of the Court and the actions of the political branches. So, physician, heal thyself."[134]

Doctors themselves seem to take the proverb as serious advice. "Physician, heal thyself," is the title of an article about doctor who got himself hooked on drugs and then got himself off. It's also the straightforward advice of Prof. Desmond O'Neill: "Physician, heal thyself...The old saying that 'the cobbler's children are never shod' holds particularly true for medicine."[135]

But author Trina Larsen Soles takes an adverse position: "'Physician heal thyself' is terrible advice. We need to look after each other and not be afraid or ashamed to seek help." Soles was distraught over a physician friend who committed suicide,[136] having not sought advice, support, or treatment from other doctors amidst his deepening depression.

---

[133]Christopher Carosa, 27 Jun 2018 (https://www.benefitspro.com/2018/06/27/physician- heal-thyself-advisor-advise-thyself-caro/?slreturn=20190013210749)
[134]Sen Chuck Grassley, (R) Iowa Aug 5 2016.
[135]Desmond Oneill, "Physician Heal Thyself" (http://workwell.ie/physician-heal-thyself/July 2018) Accessed 13 Jan 2019.
[136]Trina Larsen Soles, 7 May 2018 (https://vancouversun.com/opinion/op-ed/trina-larsen-soles-physician-heal-thyself-is-terrible-advice in Vancouver Sun).

Poor and needy

Like "rich and powerful," "poor and needy" is a blanket term. It is so general it doesn't identify the people it designates or the actual needs that any rational person or government would agree demand response. However, its brevity invites the hearer or reader to apply the term himself. The phrase occurs more than a dozen times in the Bible.

Psalm 86:1 "Bow down thine ear, O LORD, hear me: for I am poor and needy."

Many of the poor and needy are in the third world. A letter in *The* (Malaysia) *Star* in 2013 argued for financial aid to the poor and needy: "Recently, [the] former Prime Minister made a call to stop giving annual cash handouts...to the lower-income group. His reason is that it will make them lazier. My contention is that the very fact they belong to the lower-income group is simply because they are poor—it's not their choice— and in dire need of financial help." The writer engaged in the logical fallacy of tautology: they're in the lower income class because they're poor—i.e. "they're poor because they're poor." We understand the heartfelt core of his argument. But what *makes* them poor? That's what governments have to figure out, so they can treat the disease, not just the symptoms.[137]

"Privatisation harms poor and needy, says [a] UN poverty expert", "systematically eliminating human rights protections and further marginalising those living in poverty."[138] We commented briefly on this subject under "No man can serve two masters."

---

[137](https://www.thestar.com.my/opinion/letters/2013/10/05/help-the-poor-and-needy/#vsP4O7iphHsZuMihD.99)

[138]Editors, Posted Oct 24, 2018 (https://mronline.org/2018/10/24/privatisation-harms-poor-and-needy-says-un-poverty-expert)

For those who firmly believe that lawyers are in the "rich and powerful" camp and bilk the helpless populace of money it doesn't have, this from Malaysia: "Chief Justice Richard Malanjum today suggested that lawyers ...represent 20 cases per year involving poor and needy individuals to allow them access to justice."[139] In the States, of course, it's the law that the poor and needy have access to free attorneys if they qualify. The courts *have to appoint* legal counsel.

But "the poor and needy" are often pitted by their alleged political champions against the "rich and powerful," who are often vaguely defined. We hear about the inequities mostly at election time. "Pew Research Center's recent report on the public's political values found that partisan differences in attitudes about aid to the poor and needy have widened considerably over the past two decades. In that study, 71% of Democrats said the government should do more to help the needy even if it meant going deeper in debt, compared with 24% of Republicans." We think that Democrats when responding to such polls have something entirely different in mind when they say "help" than do Republicans.[140]

The debate probably won't end. An author identified only as "a Conservative" wrote in *The Boston Quarterly Review, Vol IV (1841)* "You a Christian! you spending your thousands for your own gratification, steeped in selfishness, caring for the poor and needy only to use them for your own advantage, *you,* a Christian!"[141] We take it to heart.

---

[139]V. Anbalagan, in *Free Malaysia Today News,* 11 Dec 2018 (https://www.freemalaysia today.com/category/nation/2018/12/11/represent-poor-and-needy-people-too-chief-justice-te lls-lawyers/) Accessed 14 Jan 2018.
    [140]Pew Research Center, 30 Jan 2018, (http://www.people-press.org/2018/01/30/ majorities-say-government-does-too-little-for-older-people-the-poor-and-the-middle-class)
    [141] *The Boston Quarterly Reivew,* (Boston, Benjamin H. Green, 1841) 167.

Potter's field

Across the country there are plots of land, often remote and secluded, where the destitute, the homeless, criminals, and the unknown, are buried. Many of these plots bear the name, "Potter's Field." The term comes from the New Testament.

Matthew 27:7 "And they took counsel, and bought with them the potter's field, to bury strangers in."

Judas had betrayed Jesus for thirty silver coins. Overcome with guilt, he went to the chief priests and elders and threw the money back at them. Then he went out and hanged himself in the potter's field, a place outside Jerusalem where potters went to get clay. The self-righteous Jewish leaders debated what to do with the money, since it had purchased Jesus' blood. They decided to buy the field, which acquired the name *"Akeldema,"* "field of blood" in Greek. Eventually, however, the name that came into the English language was the original: Potter's Field.

"A rare look at New York City's potter's field, home to 1 million dead," says a headline in *The Morning Call.* "A small island in the waters off the Bronx that holds the remains of about 1 million deceased New Yorkers has long been shrouded in secrecy, with limited public access. …White markers of concrete or plastic piping note the location of many, but not all, of the graves. Each represents 150 souls buried below and bears a number linked to records with information about the dead."[142]

Chicago, too, has a crowded Potter's Field. The Chicago City Cemetery's potter's field, an early location and one of several such places eventually, became the resting place of 15,212 bodies between 1860 and 1866 (the Civil War) alone. At least

---

[142]Verena Dobnik, "A rare look at New York City's potter's field, home to 1 million dead" (*The Morning Call,* Allentown, PA, 24 May 2018)

3,871 of those were Confederate prisoners of war.[143]

In Cleveland, OH, is an easily missed cemetery with precious few grave markers. "Established in 1904 by the City of Cleveland, Potter's Field is the burial ground of the poor, the homeless, and those whose bodies had been unclaimed. Some were victims of crime, others were criminals themselves. Here, there is nothing to distinguish them apart."[144]

The story is eerily the same in Dauphin County, PA, where PennLive says, "Even the field where the unwanted and forgotten are buried is hardly noticeable. …The elements have long since washed the numbers from many of these crude markers, poured by county prisoners as they did hard time over the years. Without numbers, it's nearly impossible for the coroner's office to identify those buried in these plots, virtually voiding any memory of their lives."[145]

Orange County, CA, also has several potter's fields, and teams of anthropologists and students are trying to recover remains for identification through DNA, where requested. However, due to "overpopulation," so to speak, the county's strategy changed some time ago. "The Orange County Sheriff-Coroner stopped burying our John and Jane Does in the 1980s. Instead, the office collects and stores multiple samples of an unidentified body for DNA testing, and cremates what's left and scatters those ashes in the ocean."[146]

It makes people with families who love them feel grateful that they will be missed, memorialized, and remembered.

---

[143]"Hidden Truths: Potter's Field" (http://hiddentruths.northwestern.edu/potter_field.html) Accessed 14 Jan 2019.

[144]Anonymous, (http://www.deadohio.com/pottersfield.htm) Accessed 14 Jan 2019.

[145]Rebecca Jones, "Potter's Field: Burial place for the lost and forgotten" (https://www.pennlive.com/midstate/index.ssf/2014/10/potters_field_burial_place_for.html), Accessed 14 Jan 2019.

[146] Louis Casiano, "Who is buried in potter's field?" (*Orange County Register*, August 25, 2015), Accessed 14 Jan 2019.

Powers that be

As with numerous other expressions in this book, "powers that be" shows up in titles of endless media productions and print publications. But it's also used in everyday speech and writing. It retains the archaic language of its source.

Romans 13:1 "Let every soul be subject unto the higher powers. For there is no power but of God: the powers that be are ordained of God."

"The powers that be" in Paul's description is simply "the powers that exist." But "be" has a classical ring to it, and no one would think of updating the phrase.

To employ the expression, however, often implies that the speaker or writer is being cautious, diplomatic, or deliberately obscure about just what powers he's referring to. Not that the reader or hearer can't figure it out for himself.

A prison guard in HMP Humber Prison (UK) was attacked in January 2019 and left in a pool of blood. Another guard who commented "claimed the 'powers that be' were not paying attention to the concerns raised by prison guards about the state of the prison."[147] We think it's fairly obvious those powers include the warden, for one. But we're not going to get involved on this side of the pond.

In an article on Libcom.org about the newest socialist darling, Alexandria Ocasio-Cortez (D)New York, the writer is disappointed by the U.S. House's failure to pull the trigger on a bill that would have taken a first step to eliminate ICE. The author said, "Revolts occur when ordinary people can no longer tolerate living as they have been, when there is no alternative or hope in the powers that be, when there is no faith

---

[147]Tom Kershaw, in HullLive (https://www.hulldailymail.co.uk/news/hull-east-yorkshire-news/hmp-humber-prison-guard-left-2421406, 11 Jan 2019) Accessed 14 Jan 2019.

in the two parties or in social reformers with big promises that they fail to keep."[148] These "powers that be" to which the socialist writer refers are the democratically elected representatives of this country. We don't take too well to revolt, and if it comes to that, the author will do what he can to defeat the revolutionists.

(Our sincere hope is that socialists will continue to be thwarted and ultimately defeated. The *powers that be* in this country should continue to be the people, who elect leaders to swear to uphold and defend the Constitution of the United States, a democratic republic. If the *powers that be* ever become socialists, we will assume that God has ordained them to teach us a lesson that a people who abandon him will ultimately pay a terrible price.)

A professor Colin Davis of Bristol University (UK) believes in anthropocentric climate change (man-caused global warming) so much that he spray painted slogans on an environmental agency headquarters in January, 2019. His defense of himself (though he was released) is that he "doesn't think this is really about politics. He thinks it's about economics. The powers that be tell us to vote and write to local congresspeople and such, but these suggestions feel almost insulting at times. Government knows about climate change. But powerful businesses want to stay powerful, no matter how many petitions people sign."[149] We think he could start putting some solid, empirical, documented facts in his letters, instead of just throwing mud at people who disagree with him—and that's *plenty* of people, including a lot of the powers that be.

---

[148]Scott Jay, "Abolish ICE by funding it" 8 Jan 2019 (https://libcom.org/news/abolishing-ice-funding-it-07012019) Accessed 14 Jan 2019.

[149]Ilana Strauss, "This professor just got arrested for making climate change grafitti" 14 Jan 2019 (https://www.treehugger.com/climate-change/professor-just-got-arrested-making-climate-change-grafitti.html) Accessed 14 Jan 2019.

Pride goes before a fall

Perhaps second only to "money is the root of all evil," this expression is a misquoted Bible verse. It's really a shortened version of the original in the Old Testament:

Proverbs 16:18 "Pride goeth before destruction, and an haughty spirit before a fall."

The expression gets a lot of use in public forums. Everybody wants to warn the opponent that he's about to plummet. The Chinese recently leveled it against President Trump: "A Communist party-controlled newspaper has launched a searing attack on Donald Trump after the president-elect threatened a realignment of his country's policies towards China, warning the US president-elect: 'Pride goes before a fall.'"[150] We wonder what that sounds like in Chinese.

The *Ada* (OK) *News* ran an editorial in 2014 recalling Pearl Harbor and drawing a parallel to ISIS. "Following Japan's attack on Pearl Harbor, Naval Marshal General Isoroku Yamamoto is reported to have lamented, 'I fear all we have done is to awaken a sleeping giant and fill him with a terrible resolve.' ...Almost as striking as ISIS members' murderous brutality, is their complete misunderstanding of American resolve and what it portends for them. If pride goes before a fall, they're headed for a big one." We hear that Yamamoto made the remark about the sleeping giant only in the movie, *Tora, Tora, Tora*. But we hope the editor is right about ISIS. They've been cruisin' for a bruisin' for a long time. In early 2019 it looks like that "fall" is impending.[151]

---

[150]Tom Phillips, "Chinese State Tabloid warns Donald Trump, 'Pride goes before a fall,'" in *The Guardian*, 12 Dec 2016

[151]In the *Ada News*, 15 Sep 2014 (https://www.theadanews.com/opinion/editorials/for-isis-pride-goes-before-a-fall/article_68700c44-3ce1-11e4-9bd2-ff337c1c7de7.html).

Put words in one's mouth

Usually found as, "Don't put words in my mouth!" this expression is used liberally. No one likes to be accused of saying things he/she didn't. The original context is quite different.

2 Samuel 14:3 "Come to the king, and speak on this manner unto him. So Joab put the words in her mouth."

The "her" in the verse was a woman employed by Joab, a commander under King David of Israel, to go to David and tell him a story. The hope was that David would see the light and stop his excessive grieving about the death of Absalom. The troops were becoming disheartened by their king. Joab told the woman—who appears to have been a convincing actress!—what to say, spinning a story about two brothers fighting. Joab *put words in her mouth*—he wrote the script for her little play.

Today's usage is not about telling people what *to* say, but rather telling them what you presume they *are* saying. Most people are irritated by it.

"The former director of Black Outreach for George W. Bush, Paris Dennard, told CNN host Chris Cuomo …to not put words in his mouth after he defended President Donald Trump's Charlottesville remarks. Cuomo took issue with Dennard defending Trump's comments and accused Dennard of 'straining' to make his point. This prompted Dennard to tell Cuomo, 'I'm not straining Chris. It's not strained. Trust me it's not strained. Don't put words in my mouth,' he said on 'New Day' Wednesday."[152] Frankly, we think more presumptuous interviewers would get put in their place like that.

---

[152]Nick Givas, *The Daily Caller* 23 Aug 2017 (https://dailycaller.com/2017/08/23/cnns-chris-cuomo-slapped-down-by-guest-dont-put-words-in-my-mouth-video/)

Put your house in order

We've always found horoscopes to be an odd obsession with some people. The idea that the stars have anything at all to do with personal character, behavior, or human events strikes us as somewhere between naive and ludicrous. And the daily horoscope advice sounds pretty much like the rambling of a carnival fortune teller. We don't read them, never have. But one came up in a search for our phrase of this page. It was for Aquarius, in 2012:

Family talks may get a little combative. You can make wonderful contributions to any organization that you join. You can make it up to them later. You need time to put your house in order and sort out what you are going to do about your personal direction.

We defy anyone to deny that this advice could apply to anyone at any time of the year. Note the part about putting your house in order. Who doesn't need that? Perhaps someone with extreme excessive compulsive disorder (OCD). But even they would try to put it *even more* in order.

"Put your house in order" appears more than a dozen times in the Old Testament.

2 Kings 20:1 "In those days was Hezekiah sick unto death. And the prophet Isaiah the son of Amoz came to him, and said unto him, Thus saith the Lord, Set thine house in order; for thou shalt die, and not live."

One can certainly put (or sometimes, "get") his house in order literally. J. J. O'Donoghue (special to the *Japan Times*) advises reading a "phenomenal" book by Marie Kondo because it "can help put your house in order" — Kondo is a cleaning consultant. Many a homemaker has thought about having somebody come in and help get everything organized, and downsized.

But the usual use of the phrase has to do with logistics, situations, relationships, business practices and the like.

We remember a 2008 episode of CBS's "NCIS" in which the newly installed director of the agency, Leon Vance, was being addressed by the Secretary of the Navy, amidst swirling events of internal turmoil. The secretary cut the small talk and turned serious: "When the vacancy was created at the top of your agency, you induced me to give you this post. The deal was simple: Get your house in order!"[153]

Closest to the word given to Hezekiah is advice like The Summit Medical Group gives on its website: "Resolve to put your house in order with advance directives. Advance directives are written, legal instructions regarding your preferences for medical care if you are unable to make decisions for yourself." Good advice. When Hezekiah was told to put his order and then got the bad news he was going to die, he cried and prayed, and he got fifteen more years from the Lord. Any of us might not be so blessed.

---

[153]Jesse Stern,"Cloak" in NCIS SE6 E8, (2008)

Quick and the dead

This expression barely made the main book listings, owing to its infrequent use except in book, movie, music and band titles. It does show up now and then, however. It comes from Paul.

2 Timothy 4:1 "I charge thee therefore before God, and the Lord Jesus Christ, who shall judge the quick and the dead at his appearing and his kingdom."

In King James's day, "quick" meant "living." The Greek word behind "quick" is nothing more than the common one in Koine Greek for people who are alive. By the time Hollywood got hold of the expression, however, "quick" was taken to mean "fast," and it was logical to assume that gunfighters, if they wanted not to be dead, had to be quick.

That's the sense most people who appropriate "quick and the dead" use when applying it to entertainment offerings.

Cruzbike.com is a forum for owners of the oddly designed but very fast Cruzbike Recumbent Bicycle, used principally for racing. A user on the forum started a discussion he called, "The quick and the dead: a discussion in Cruzebikes at speed." The user took the expression the way most people do these days. It's inaccurate, but English is what it is.

Stone Payton, one of the hosts of the radio program "High Velocity Business Radio," makes a career out of "helping others produce better results in less time." His book title says it all, *SPEED®: Never Fry Bacon In The Nude: And Other Lessons From The Quick & The Dead.*[154]

---

[154](https://businessradiox.com/wp-content/uploads/2017/09/HighVelocity.jpg)

Reap the whirlwind

This phrase comes from one of the minor prophets of the Old Testament.

Hosea 8:7 "For they have sown the wind, and they shall reap the whirlwind."

The 2018 nomination of Brett Kavanaugh to the U.S. Supreme Court was fiercely contested in the Senate during confirmation hearings. The opposition included reputation-ruining charges that were never substantiated, but Kavanaugh was confirmed. In addressing the Senate Judiciary Committee about the entire process, Kavanaugh said Democrats had "sowed the wind, for decades to come." He added he feared "the whole country will reap the whirlwind."[155] We believe he was prescient, and we shudder to think what winds may come.

Using their own scriptures against them, the Mexican Ambassador to the U. N. said recently, "El Estado de Israel continúa sembrando vientos y continuará cosechando tempestades." You can easily guess what that says.

In 2016, the UK voted to leave the EU. Former foreign secretary Boris Johnson, tired of all the delays and attempts by the UK's own "deep state" to reverse Brexit, said, "If we think that by coming up with all kinds of complicated amendments and delaying tactics, we are going to fool the British public, we will manage to frustrate Brexit, I think we will reap the whirlwind." We agree. A voting public can be pushed so far until they elect a maverick who will actually do what he campaigns on doing.

---

[155]Richard A. Arenberg, "Who will reap the whirlwind on Kavanaugh?" 1 Oct 2018 (https://www.newsmax.com/richardarenberg/kavanaugh-supreme-court-accusations-fbi/20 18/10/01/id/884268), Accessed 15 Jan 2019.

Red sky at night, shepherds' delight

Matthew 16:2-3 "He answered and said unto them, When it is evening, ye say, It will be fair weather: for the sky is red. And in the morning, It will be foul weather to day: for the sky is red and lowring. O ye hypocrites, ye can discern the face of the sky; but can ye not discern the signs of the times?"

Jesus was upbraiding the Pharisees and Sadducees for their stubbornness, since they refused to believe in him, replete though his ministry was with signs of his identity. In fact, they asked for a sign. His observation was that they could read the weather but they wouldn't recognize him when it was as plain as the nose on their face.

"Red sky at night," etc., probably predated Jesus, but in English the saying was popularized by the Bible.

We've always heard the other version, "Red sky at night, sailors' delight; red sky at morning, sailors take warning." We suppose our exposure to sheep herding wasn't sufficient to learn the lingo. Of course, it's more generally farmers' lingo.

The operative question is whether the saying is based in fact. It seems it is, at least in part. It has a lot to do with dust particles trapped in high pressure, bands of clouds along fronts, and whether those clouds are coming or going.

Whimsical variations exist. There's the farmer who recited the old saw as: "Red sky at night, shepherds delight; red sky at dawn—barn's on fire."

And then there's Tom Parry's version: "Red sky at night, shepherds' delight; blue sky at night—day."[156] Of course, that might not be true in the upper stretches of Alaska. But Jesus' comments about unbelief were perfectly on target.

---

[156] Tom Parry is an English comedian, playwright and actor.

Rise and shine

What child—at least in the author's generation and before—hasn't heard, as the first words of the day, "Rise and shine!" Parents for many years have tried, not always at first successfully, to get their children out of bed with this lights-on, noise-making, curtain-opening, blinds-raising, voice-raising announcement.

It didn't quite carry that meaning in its original context, but very, very close.

Isaiah 60:1, "Arise, shine, for your light has come, and the glory of the LORD rises upon you."

The passage in Isaiah was highly messianic. The prophet foresaw the coming of the messiah, the suffering servant, the deliverer, the king to end all kings, and he envisioned the divine invitation to Israel to rise in its attention, its devotion, its readiness for its messiah, and its realization of its calling to radiate the light of God's glory to the world. All that in two little words!

If only we could imitate that in the groggy fog of what most of us feel in the morning!

Rise & Shine appears in business and group names: a diner; a hair salon; a video sales company; a breakfast club; a catering company; a steak and egg place (which always helps *us* rise and shine); a casino; an academy; a meal program; a bakery (we can smell it now!); a delivery service; Dollywood cabins; a Pilates studio; a Behr paint (go figure); a bluegrass band; and a burger joint.

Root of the matter

Job 19:28 "But ye should say, Why persecute we him, seeing the root of the matter is found in me?"

Job's "friends" tried numerous ways to get Job to admit that God was punishing him for some specific sin and that he wouldn't recover—his health and everything he had lost—until he identified that sin and confessed it. We know from reading the whole book that Job was right to deny what they claimed. In 19:28 he leveled a criticism at them for their failure to empathize. The KJV is a bit hard to decipher. We think the CEV gets it just right when it translates the verse: "My friends, you think up ways to blame and torment me, saying I brought it on myself."

Nevertheless, "root of the matter" came over into English as an expression meaning the central part or cause of something.

Midwest Psychological Services invites interested persons to discover why they are depressed. Depression is widespread in this day and time. Where is it all coming from? Some is partly feigned, but we are living in troubled times, and true, clinical depression doesn't just happen "out of the blue." MPS tells us that "The possibilities are endless, but a depression therapist can help you get to the root of the matter."

Psychologists try to help us figure out what's at the root of the matter *inside* our heads. But, at least for black women, there's a book to help them understand what's at the root of the matter *on the outside of* their heads. *The Root Of The Matter A Natural Hair Self Help Guide,* by Lori Lindsey, offers hair growth and cycles, then gives tutorials in various hairstyles.

Now if there were just a miracle cure that got to the root of the matter for bald men.

Safe and sound

Luke 15:27 "And he said unto him, Thy brother is come; and thy father hath killed the fatted calf, because he hath received him safe and sound."

Coming from the parable of the prodigal son, "safe and sound" is in absolutely everyone's personal vocabulary. The English phrase was used to translate the Greek word *hugiainonta,* meaning "whole," or "in good health. Of course, the prodigal son's family didn't have any idea where he had been while he was gone, so the word communicated the idea assigned to it by the KJV translators: both *safe* and *sound (or healthy)*.

"I'm back, safe and sound," the author has been known to say after hundreds of miles of travel on his motorcycle, his wife at home not exactly worried but eager to know that nothing bad had happened to him.

One description of what an OnStar vehicle plan does for a new car owner is reassuring: "OnStar, 1-year of Safe and Sound plan Includes Automatic Crash Notification, Automatic Notification of Air Bag Deployment, Stolen Vehicle Location Assistance, [and] a link to all Emergency Services." It sounds like when you hear from OnStar at home, it doesn't *quite* mean that all is well. It's more like what you would hear if you got that phone call you hoped you wouldn't get, but the voice at the other end says, "I'm all right; but there's been a little accident."

And finally, the week this entry was written the U.S. was abuzz with the story that Jayme Kloss, a Barron, WI, teen abducted from her home after an intruder shot her parents dead, had escaped him after eighty-eight days and was "safe and sound." Well, there is some good news in the news, after all.

Salt of the earth

Matthew 5:13 "Ye are the salt of the earth"

In this verse from the Sermon on the Mount, Jesus told his hearers—prospectively his followers—that they were the intermediary sources of God's preserving grace in the world. Jesus meant that people who follow him are the conduit of his word that reveals him and his salvation to every generation.

The expression that comes down into English doesn't hold quite that meaning, as with many other phrases derived from the Bible. "Salt of the earth" tends to mean "just plain, good folks." The author's brother in a funeral sermon once described a church member as "just a salt-of-the-earth kind of guy."

Hillary Clinton was roundly (and deservedly) criticized in the 2016 election for calling Donald Trump's supporters "deplorables." It was a thoroughly elitist comment that revealed something about her that was not complimentary. Said one person, "The targets of Hillary's ire are, by and large, the salt of the earth, whose only real sin was opposing her corrupt candidacy."[157]

An interviewer talking with a co-director of the film, *Hillbilly,* said that in describing people in coal country, "there's this stereotype…that they're all poor and uneducated with crooked teeth," but on the other hand "that they're salt of the earth white working class."[158]

Maybe the Bible phrase and our phrase aren't so far apart. As Paul wrote, "Brothers and sisters, consider your calling: Not many were wise from a human perspective, not many powerful, not many of noble birth" (1 Corinthians 1:26, CSV).

---

[157](https://www.americanthinker.com/blog/2019/01/deplorable_or_unjustly_deplored.html)

[158](https://climateone.org/audio/summer-films-corn-coal-lights-and-flights)

Scapegoat

A scapegoat is someone who takes the blame for someone else or for a larger group, of which he or she may also be a part in wrongdoing. The scapegoat need not be guilty himself, however. In fact, that circumstance would better fit the origin of this phrase, from the writings of Moses.

Leviticus 16:10 "But the goat, on which the lot fell to be the scapegoat, shall be presented alive before the LORD, to make an atonement with him, and to let him go for a scapegoat into the wilderness."

The English "Scapegoat" comes from "escape" and "goat," obviously, and it literally means a goat allowed to escape (into the wilderness). The goat of Leviticus symbolically bore the sins of the people and when he disappeared, they were free of them.

In Christian theology, Jesus fulfilled that symbolism, through his death on the cross. Because of the meaning found in both the Pentateuch and the Gospel, "scapegoat" has come to mean someone who takes the punishment someone else deserves.

A close synonym is "patsy," though that word usually implies someone who is easily deceived as well. Lee Harvey Oswald, upon learning that he had been accused of killing President Kennedy, blurted out with dejection, "Well, I'm the patsy." Many people believe that Oswald did not shoot Kennedy, that at least two other people did, that the "shooter's nest" in the Texas School Book Depository was a set up, and that Oswald was the scapegoat, taking the blame for what others, who may never be identified, did.

See the light

Contrary to a logical argument that "see the light" is independent of the Bible for its source, we argue that even though the explicit meaning of the words could easily have arisen apart from any major writing, the semi-symbolic usage of the words owes its persistence in modern English to the Bible.

Luke 11:33 "No man, when he hath lighted a candle, putteth it in a secret place, neither under a bushel, but on a candlestick, that they which come in may see the light.

Jesus was talking about influence, about evangelism, about living openly and boldly for the Lord. The light symbolizes these things.

We can't help but think of James Brown, as The Reverend Cleophus Brown in the *The Blues Brothers*. He reaches the high point of his sermon and points toward where Jake and Elwood Blues stand, Jake bathed in light streaming from the stained glass windows above the choir. Brown shouts, "Do you see the light?!" And the third time he calls out, Jake shouts, "Yes! I see the light!" In that moment he knows he is supposed to re-form "the band." As they are later to say several times, "We're on a mission from God."

The scene, of course, is comedic, but it's based on a very serious truth imparted to everyone who becomes a follower of Jesus Christ. He is expected to discern and do the will of God for his/her life. That responsibility is summarized well by what Jesus said: "See the light." Then do what it says.

This use of "see the light" is distinct from "see the light of day" or "see the light and feel the heat," both of which use the symbolism for something other than the recognition of truth.

Seek and ye shall find

Matthew 7:7 "Ask, and it shall be given you; seek, and ye shall find; knock, and it shall be opened unto you."

Most people who use the phrase, "Seek and ye (or you) shall find are deliberately employing the scriptural expression, with knowledge of its source, to validate their purposeful, persistent search for something, be it an answer, an object, a position, or whatever.

A documentation manager for Nexpose (https://www.rapid7 .com/products/nexpose) writes: "Seek and you shall find—information! Nothing frustrates me more than searching online for something I desperately need to put out a fire, and getting tons of results...except for that one critical nugget that I'm looking for. ...We're revamping our search in Nexpose Help for a future release so that you can find what you need quickly, without a lot of digging." Nothing like helping along the divine promise.

BreastCancerTrials.wordpress.com says in its 14 May 2014 blog, Seek and you shall find. For some time, BCT users have been telling us that what they'd most like to see on BCT is a search box. Well, I'm excited to let you know that the BCT Search Box is now live on our website." We might suggest that those concerned about breast cancer are also well advised to conduct self-examinations. We hope that in seeking they will not also find, but it's better to find and fight than not seek, and then succumb.

Then there's the Smokey Mountain Zipline, which advertises, "In search of relaxation? Seek and you shall find it in the Smokies!" (https://www.smokymountainziplines.com /blog/ziplines/in-search-of-relaxation-seek-and-you-shall-fin d-it-in-the-smokies.php). Their site shows a couple being massaged. We think we'll stick with that and skip the ziplines.

Sign of the times

Matthew 16:3 "O ye hypocrites, ye can discern the face of the sky; but can ye not discern the signs of the times?"

"Signs of the times," was Jesus' expression for the indications that any devoted Jew should have been able to read to see what God was doing and was about to do in their generation.

In modern English, the saying is rendered mostly in the singular, and it doesn't usually refer to God's working but rather to some practice, pursuit, or development that is emblematic of the culture or the times in which we live.

Jon Chesto of *The Boston Globe* (November 28, 2018) says "UTC [United Technologies Corp.], GE breakups are a sign of the times." Not just breaking up, but recombining: "The conglomerate is dead. Long live the conglomerate!"

Blogger Nathan Winograd (www.nathanwinograd.com) gives us some details about Michigan's stats on euthanizing animals, saying that from nearly 120,000 animals in 2007, the number was down in 2016 to 29,591. Nathan opines–and we heartily agree—"If Michigan is a sign of the times, it is good news for the No Kill movement." Nathan posted an endearing picture of a cat that looks like one of the author's two. Aww!

A staff writer for JLL Realviews says of downtown businesses, "All buildings need a refresh from time to time. But when scaffolding goes up, retailers are often faced with uncertainty and the prospect of lost trade." That's why "scaffolding is a sign of the times for retailers."[159] And it comes at a price. Who wants to walk under scaffolding to go in a store? Isn't that just as ill advised as walking under a ladder?

---

[159]5 Oct 2018 (https://www.jllrealviews.com/industries/retail/scaffolding-sign-times-retailers/)

Skin of one's teeth

English contains a number of idioms using the properties of skin to express other ideas. We say something gets under our skin, meaning either to irritate, which is negative, or to deeply affect, which can be positive. We say someone has thin skin, meaning they're too prone to take offense. We say someone has thick skin, meaning they can take a lot of criticism without getting mad or quitting. And we say, "It's no skin off my nose," meaning it won't affect or bother me.[160] "By the skin of [one's] teeth" draws on the property of skin that it's a covering designed to protect.

The source of the phrase is the Old Testament, in a book that probably traces—in its oral tradition, anyway—to the period of the patriarchs, the lifetimes of Abraham, Isaac and Jacob, somewhere earlier than 1,500 B.C.

Job 19:20 "My bone cleaveth to my skin and to my flesh, and I am escaped with the skin of my teeth."

The Geneva Bible, which preceded the King James by half a century, rendered the Hebrew of Job, "*by* the skin of my teeth." To escape either "by" or "with" the skin of one's teeth is to escape with one's life, but only barely. Teeth, of course, have no skin. They do have enamel, a layer that can be worn away by drinking Coca-Cola too frequently, as we're warned by people selling toothpaste and mouthwash—which doesn't make it any less true. But if teeth had skin, it would be frightfully thin. The wry observation by Old Testament Job is therefore all the more effective.

Sometimes a writer will employ tooth skin more positively,

---

[160]Famously, Mr. Reineman, a character in *It's a Wonderful Life,* says to Mr. Potter, the villain in that film, "Look, Mr. Potter, it's no skin off my nose. I'm just your little rent collector. But you can't laugh off this Bailey Park any more."

not as escape but rather as narrowly succeeding. Language Systems, the International College of English, wrote a little dialogue for students in which "Alfonso" tells "Laurie, " I ran to the bus stop, and it was already there, and I barely caught it by the skin of my teeth."

Emily Bennett, a Michigan woman who clearly likes beer, set a goal to go to every Michigan brewery within a year. She started in Grand Rapids and ended in Detroit, traveling about 12,000 miles. She visited 323 places, including the Gravel Bottom Craft Brewery in Ada, Michigan, where being interviewed about her accomplishment, she revealed that she used up her year, but "I did make it—by the skin of my teeth."[161]

The less figurative phrase, "a narrow escape," is hardly as evocative, but it means the same thing. So does "another coat of paint," as in, "Another coat of paint and that car would have hit me!"

---

[161]Gary Stoller, "By the Skin of Her Teeth, A Michigan Woman Visits Every Craft Brewery in the State" (https://www.forbes.com/sites/garystoller/2018/07/11/by-the-skin-of-her-teeth-a-michigan-woman-visits-every-craft-brewery-in-the-state/#11f513275f81) Accessed 4 Jan 2019.

Sour grapes

Ezekiel 18:2 "What mean ye, that ye use this proverb concerning the land of Israel, saying, The fathers have eaten sour grapes, and the children's teeth are set on edge?"

The proverb expressed bitterness over the perception that ancestors' sins hurt their descendants more than themselves. God told Ezekiel that he didn't punish children for their parents' sins. Nevertheless, people's sins often have far reaching consequences not erased by forgiveness.

"Sour grapes" are often plucked from the original proverb and used by themselves to mean a distasteful experience. Some people think "sour grapes" means just resentment or envy.

A woman asked a money manager what she could do about suspected fiduciary abuse by a sibling who had had power of attorney for their father. She said, "I don't mean for this to come across as sour grapes." We think she meant resentment of the sibling's authority to manage the father's affairs.

Georgeann King of *Midtown Republican* has tried to make sense of Mitt Romney. In a blunt assessment opening her article, "Catch this, Mitt" (4 Jan 2019, http://midtown republican.com/ archives/21137) she writes: "My opinion of Mitt Romney has changed over the years. When he lost the Republican nomination to John McCain in 2008, I thought he was a classy guy with a future. When he lost the general election to Barack Obama in 2012, I thought he was a good man with a glass jaw. When he repeatedly got on his high horse to sabotage Donald Trump's presidential campaign in 2016, I thought he was an opportunistic sleaze bag gorging on sour grapes and his own monstrously selfish sense of virtue." She means "bitterness" by "sour grapes." And boy, what a fastball that summation was!

Spare the rod, spoil the child

It isn't politically correct to quote this proverb in any context meaning to recommend parental discipline (but then, what *isn't* politically incorrect these days?). But it's ancient wisdom.

Proverbs 13:24 "He that spareth his rod hateth his son: but he that loveth him chasteneth him betimes."

The recommendation of this verse is joined by Proverbs 29:15 in using the word "rod," and Proverbs 23:13 and others in talking about employing some form of discipline. The Bible doesn't mince words about parents' needing to discipline their children, and about folly being bound up in the heart of a child (Proverbs 22:15). The casual reader of the Bible shouldn't jump to the conclusion that the Bible means to beat children. It doesn't. A switch is sufficient. Even more, parents should devise forms of discipline suited to situations, that teach children that deliberate disobedience and rebellion have painful consequences.

This is the meaning of the proverb today, though it is used sometimes by the ungodly to justify the unloving. Because it is, it is therefore sometimes used by the irreligious to condemn religion. We suspect that things will continue to be this way until God brings judgment on the world — proving that sin *will* be punished eventually, even if some parents won't do it now.

The actual form of today's expression, "Spare the rod, spoil the child," comes from a 17th century poem by Samuel Butler, "Hudibras," in which Butler mocked religious fanatics of his day. The couplet is: "Love is a boy by poets styl'd, Then spare the rod, and spoil the child." Butler's phrasing was iambic and used repeating sibilance, fitting it for English poetry. But his source was undoubtedly one or both of the verses quoted above.

Spirit is willing but the flesh is weak

It is predictable that craft distillers would make use of the first part of this expression. However, one writer made use of the whole phrase to condemn student drinking.

The expression was spoken by Jesus, who, during his experience in Gethsemane before the crucifixion, found his disciples sleeping instead of joining him in prayer.

Matthew 26:41 "Watch and pray, that ye enter not into temptation: the spirit indeed is willing, but the flesh is weak."

Most writers get the gist all right, but usually apply the expression to other than spiritual matters. Colin Macilwain writing for *Nature, the International Journal of Science,* titles an article "U.S. spirit is willing, but the funds are still weak." (*Nature,* vol. 397, 7–8, 7 January 1999).

Marion Scott, a dancer, choreographer, and UCLA professor, revived her dancing career after years of using a walker. She had hip replacement surgeries and other treatment and got back on stage. At 84 (in 2007), "the spirit is willing," and she said only death would keep her from performing.[162]

Some wag who apparently had some sort of water sports in mind posted a picture of himself from behind, sitting atop a railing and looking over a channel of water extending out into the distance. The caption was, "The spirit is willing, but the canal is frozen."

Another guy, invited to go out with the gang for pizza, responded, "The spirit is willing, but the wallet is weak." Amen to that.

---

[162]Susan Josephs, "The spirit is willing" 8 Apr 2007 (http://articles.latimes.com/2007/apr/08/entertainment/ca-scott8) Accessed 16 Jan 2019.

Strain at a gnat, swallow a camel

In one of his strong indictments of the Pharisees, Jesus coined a memorable phrase.

Matthew 23:24 "Ye blind guides, which strain at a gnat, and swallow a camel."

We might say, "strain *out* a gnat," but it means the same thing. Jesus was saying the Pharisees made much of little infractions of the law—mostly their *own* laws—and totally missed the fact that they were ignoring and violating the great laws of God.

The criticism is especially applicable to people who tend to be legalistic, because the requirements of the small points of the law usually can be itemized, while the obligations of the "greatest commandment" and "the second, and like unto it" (Matthew 22:38-39) are not always easily quantified. The difference isn't always between the "letter" and the "spirit" of the law, but sometimes it is.

Politicians like the phrase, if they have a gnat's argument against a camel's issue. The Hon. William Irving (D-R)New York, a U.S. House of Representatives member in the early 1800s, addressed the House about supporting a bill to draft more than eighty thousand men into the army, over objections to minor issues. "It appears to me," he said, "that sometimes we strain at a gnat and swallow a camel. There is a fundamental principle in the constitution, which requires the minority, to submit to the will of the majority, constitutionally expressed, yet some in our country have forgotten *that*—" It was a nice speech. It went on for three pages and it surpassed in knowledge of history and facility with English oratory any offering the author has heard in occasional viewing of television coverage of today's Congress.

And finally, this from a Scott Tibbs, who wrote about a Bei

Bei Shuai, who was pregnant and tried to commit suicide with rat poison. She didn't die, but her baby did, and she was charged with attempted feticide. Tibbs noted that in Marion County, IN, there were 5,676 abortions in 2011. He opined: "If Shuai is convicted and punished, we can feel good that we have justice for the baby, as if that will hide our blood guilt for the 5,676 babies we have allowed to be killed last year. We strain at a gnat and swallow a camel, and that blood cannot be washed off our hands so easily."[163] That may be one of the most apropos comparisons of the gnat and the camel we have ever read.

---

[163](www.timothytibbs .com/scott/2013_archives/blog_2013_008.html)

Strait and narrow

In the golden glow of memories of youth, it seems many a movie from the 40s and 50s featured some convict being released and exhorted to walk the strait and narrow.

Matthew 7:14 "Strait is the gate, and narrow is the way, which leadeth unto life, and few there be that find it."

As opposed to the "wide" gate and "broad" road which lead to destruction," Jesus recommended the "strait and narrow." "Strait" is not "straight;" it also means narrow. (Two synonyms in a couplet are called parallelism in Hebrew poetry.) Think of the Strait of Gibralter. It's narrow. To walk the strait and narrow means to behave yourself.

Tomas Wong blogged about difficult relationships. "I know that my father hates me so I really don't care if he is proud of me or not. I have tried to walk the strait and narrow path and faltered a few times. But, at the end of the day I would like to know that my Mother was proud I was her son."[164]

A man on parole from a sentence for grand theft wrote on a forum for parolees and probationers, "I will admit that I haven't been the model probationee but one driving without a license and one failed drug test …and the judge extends it 2 yrs and adds a $5000 restitution fee. What does a man have to do to get off this leash?" Another probationer took the words out of my mouth: "Be glad he didn't revoke the probation and give you a prison sentence. Another violation and they probably will, so walk the strait and narrow and do as your probation [officer] tells you, and *obey all laws*."[165] Credit me with the emphasis.

---

[164]A comment on https://wannabegirl.org/belated-birthday-post/
[165](http://www.prisontalk.com/forums/showthread.php?t=506459)

Stranger in a strange land

"Pallid, bespectacled and with an international accent that was not quite British – but British enough – I was a stranger in a strange land where I should have belonged. We were, after all, Australian."[166] So wrote Phil Brown about his first day in high school in Queensland, AU. Phil had come from Hong Kong.

This author's vocabulary was shaped in part by his biblical upbringing, but "stranger in a strange land" wasn't in his vocabulary growing up. Apparently, it is in a few other people's. It comes from the account of the Exodus.

Exodus 2:22 "And she bare him a son, and he called his name Gershom: for he said, I have been a stranger in a strange land."

Gershom means "sojourner." The phrase has something poetic about it, which probably explains why not more people say it regularly, but which also explains why it gets into song lyrics, such as one by U2:

Stranger, stranger in a strange land.
He looked at me like I was the one who should run.
We asked him to smile for a photograph
Waited a while to see if we could make him laugh.[167]

Harriet Tubman, the famous African-American abolitionist, said after leaving the slave states into free territory, "I had crossed the line of which I had so long been dreaming. I was free; but there was no one to welcome me to the land of freedom; I was a stranger in a strange land."

---

[166](https://griffithreview.com/articles/stranger-in-a-strange-land/)
[167](https://www.u2.com/lyrics/125)

Stumbling block

1 Corinthians 1:23 "But we preach Christ crucified, unto the Jews a stumblingblock, and unto the Greeks foolishness."

"Stumblingblock" also appears in Leviticus 19:14. We selected the New Testament location because of the figurative sense. Paul said that the crucifixion was something the Jews just couldn't seem to get past and go on to place faith in the one who was crucified. In that sense, they stumbled over it.

A stumbling block, in modern English, retains almost all the sense it had in the New Testament; it's often a reference to a problem that crops up and delays or ends plans or processes.

Keith Kloor wrote an article about the climate change debate. "Kloor cites other reports that state most people aren't concerned with climate change because they don't see it affecting them in the near future. Kloor calls this a 'stumbling block' to actually solving climate change."[168] The other stumbling block is clear and convincing evidence.

"Adriana Doyle, a family attorney and mediator, once wrote: 'The only difference between stumbling blocks and stepping stones is the way in which we use them.' All successful mediators excel by taking just that approach: for every stumbling block that appears, the mediator will reposition it, shifting and turning until the step stone appears."[169]

"The difference between a stumbling block and a stepping stone is how high you raise your foot." —Benny Lewis

---

[168](https://asunow.asu.edu/content/scientific-and-public-consensus-over-climate-change-stumbling-block)

[169](https://www.lexisnexis.com/university/course.aspx?classInfo=Crs~686~20247) Accessed 16 Jan 2019.

Suffer fools (gladly)

Sometimes seen as "suffer fools gladly" and other times simply "suffer fools," this old expression comes from the pen of the Apostle Paul.

2 Corinthians 11:19 "For ye suffer fools gladly, seeing ye yourselves are wise."

First, we have to re-translate "suffer." In King James English "suffer" meant to allow, tolerate, accommodate or simply to let. In Paul's directions to the Corinthian church, he was indulging in a bit of didactic sarcasm, parroting the boasting of the Corinthian Christians who thought they were so godly for being tolerant of everyone. When he said, "Ye suffer fools gladly," he was saying they accommodated foolish people as if their folly didn't need any reproof. It was a theological version of the absurd trend in education which has it that a student who says two plus two equals five should be praised instead of shown the light.

Consequently, "You suffer fools gladly" was not a compliment. It was a serious indictment of toleration run amok. Surprisingly, however, the expression in modern English doesn't always resemble Paul's usage.

Sadie Stein, in the 16 May 2016 *Paris Review*, says, "I feel sorry for people who don't suffer fools. They're missing out on so much! The quotidian, absurd human comedy; several of Shakespeare's finest characters; TV. ...Imagine if you didn't suffer fools! What would you do for fun? I suffer them gladly, jubilantly, joyously." It deserves notice that Stein was talking about people who make fools of themselves, not so much those who make a fool of you.

David Brooks, of the *New York Times*, wrote a piece for the 3 Jan 2013 online edition on the subject of this very idiom. He said:

Today, the phrase is often used as an ambiguous compliment. It suggests that a person is so smart he has trouble tolerating people who are far below his own high standards. It is used to describe a person who is so passionately committed to a vital cause that he doesn't have time for social niceties toward those idiots who stand in its way. It is used to suggest a level of social courage; a person who has the guts to tell idiots what he really thinks.[170]

Brooks went on to say that while he doesn't put up with fools, he does try to avoid them, but he "compliments" some who are more tolerant, such as ministers. Martin Marty, a longtime resource for the theological community, took issue with that implication—somewhat. Marty wrote, "I think he sees pastors and great teachers accepting the need to suffer fools as part of their vocation...The [gospel] which imparts credentials to pastors teaches them to see people, foolish people, from a different perspective than they naturally would." Marty's point was that pastors, of all people, should be exceedingly patient toward "people abandoned, often unjustly, in an impersonal world where someone, someone, should not lose patience or become impolite and dismissive."[171]

Sometimes humorists say it compactly:

"Suffer fools gladly; they may be right" —Holbrook Jackson

"I don't suffer fools gladly, but I do gladly make fools suffer." —Anne Taintor

---

[170](https://www.nytimes.com/2013/01/04/opinion/brooks-suffering-fools-gladly.html)

[171]Martin E. Marty, "Pastors Suffer Fools" 7 Jan 2013 (https://divinity.uchicago.edu /sightings/pastors-suffer-fools-martin-e-marty) Accessed 17 Jan 2019.

Sufficient unto the day (is the evil thereof)

Like "suffer fools," "sufficient unto the day" often has the end lopped off, or replaced with something other than "evil." Usually the writer or speaker knows where it came from and quotes it as a proverb, as opposed to working it into his thoughts like an idiom. The expression comes from the Bible (as if you were surprised by now).

Matthew 6:34 "Take therefore no thought for the morrow: for the morrow shall take thought for the things of itself. Sufficient unto the day is the evil thereof."

Jesus' teaching is sometimes misunderstood—imagine that! "'Sufficient unto the day is the evil thereof' is terrible advice," wrote someone. "Clearly, you should never put off until tomorrow something you can do today."[172] The writer thought Jesus was saying not to plan or prepare—in other words, to procrastinate. She should have known better than that. Jesus was saying not to be worried or anxious. We hit at this meaning when we advise ourselves and others to "take it one day at a time" or to "live in the moment."

Other people seem to enjoy just appropriating the scriptural reference lightly and using it to introduce other ideas:

"Sufficient unto the day is one baby," said Mark Twain in "The Babies Speech" in 1879. "As long as you are in your right mind don't you ever pray for twins. Twins amount to a permanent riot; and there ain't any real difference between triplets and a insurrection."

According to Ian Alexander, "Sufficient unto the day are the apples thereof." Says he, "Everyone who has ever owned an

---

[172] Author unknown (https://www.pressreader.com/usa/daily-press/20181208/282011853440634)

Apple tree knows the problem. Monday: Apple Pie. Tuesday: Stewed Apple. Wednesday: Oh, Stewed Apple again, no time for baking. Thursday: Apple Crumble. Friday: Stewed Apple. Saturday: Freeze some stewed apple. Sunday: Roast Pork with Apple Sauce. And so on with Apple Charlotte, Apple Cake, Roast Chicken with Apple Sauce, etc." He was speaking with tongue in cheek—somewhat. Clearly he likes apples. The author's wife loves apples, and in season we ride into the nearby mountains and get a number of them sufficient for each day until they run out—or rot.[173]

Peter Arango, writing for A Medium Corporation on 19 Dec 2017, summarized the saying well: "As a lad I was told, 'sufficient unto the day is the evil thereof,' a convoluted reminder that there's trouble enough without inventing problems." We would add only, 'or imagining them.' That's precisely what Jesus was talking about.[174]

---

[173]Ian Alexander, 5 September 2015, (http://www.obsessedbynature.com/blog/2015/09/05/sufficient-unto-the-day-are-the-apples-thereof/) Accssed 17 Jan 2019.
[174]Peter Arango, "How are you today?" (https://medium.com/@parango46/how-are-you-today-c26b4a7b8cb8)

Sweat of your brow

Genesis 3:19 "In the sweat of thy face shalt thou eat bread, till thou return unto the ground…"

Interestingly, "sweat of your brow" is not the wording of the KJV in Genesis; "brow" replaced "face" later. When multiple other translations came along, most of them picked up the "brow" language. The NIV, HCSB, ISV and many others have "brow," reflecting the more widely used version of the saying. It makes little difference, if any. The idea is still the same. As the CEV puts it: "You will sweat all your life to earn a living." Most translations also render the first word "By" rather than "with," which also makes no difference; it's just consistent with modern English. But speakers and writers often, if not usually, quote no more of the Bible verse than, "sweat of your brow," and often that's "sweat of my brow," or some other pronoun.

Says a columnist in the *Roanoke Star*: "I've been fertilizing my land with the sweat of my brow and was gardening long before gardening was cool. …Eating local wasn't hip and trendy, it was cheap and healthy; and a carbon footprint was what happened when I stepped in the ashes from the wood stove.[175] And Mike Summey says in a book on investing: "If you can walk away from the showroom thinking, 'Wow, I would love to have that car, but not now. I'm an investor; I spend money only on things that will show me a return. I will wait to own that car until I can pay for it from my investment earnings rather than from the sweat of my brow.' Now, my friend, you are thinking like an investor!"[176]

---

[175]Jeff Ell, "No Till Gardening – Or How Not To Garden Like A Heathen" 10 July 2015 (http://theroanokestar.com/2015/07/10/no-till-gardening-or-how-not-to-garden-like-a-heathen) Accessed 17 Jan 2019.
[176]Mike Summey, *Financial Security Bible,* (Gildan Media LLC, 2018)

Sweeter than honey

Our guess is that if you counted the song lyrics that contain this phrase, you would fill a page in this book with the titles. The phrase *is* the title of a number of songs, including one by Southside Johnny & the Asbury Jukes, another by Marc Isaacs, one by Jefferson Starship, and another by Jackie Lomax. The altogether likely source of "sweeter than honey" in English is the Bible.

Judges 14:18 "And the men of the city said unto him on the seventh day before the sun went down, What is sweeter than honey? and what is stronger than a lion?"

The phrase appears also in Psalm 19:10 and Psalm 119:103. It needs no explanation, does it? In the references in the Psalms the phrase refers to the word and truths of God. In Judges it was the answer to a riddle posed by Samson. In modern music, it's often a reference to a lover's lips or affection.

A writer for Maple From Canada asked the question quite literally, whether maple syrup is sweeter than honey. (We paid attention to this one because we go through *a lot* of maple syrup.) He answered his own question by looking at a chart that showed that by volume maple syrup has 54 grams of sugars to honey's 71 — so it's *not* sweeter than honey. (But it's better on toast.) However, maple syrup has vastly more manganese, riboflavin, zinc, magnesium, calcium, and potassium than honey. And either of these two natural products way outshines cane sugar, which has practically nothing but, well, *sugar*. (After all, that's all it's supposed to have in it.)

And, we thought we'd heard some "way out there" names for churches, until we came across the "Sweeter Than Honey Church," in Tyler, TX.

Tearing my hair out

It seemed to us that this phrase might not be from the Bible until we looked into the matter at some length. It seems that even some hair specialists think it probably originated with Ezra.

Ezra 9:3 "And when I heard this thing, I rent my garment and my mantle, and plucked off the hair of my head and of my beard, and sat down astonied."

Lord Hair company says in its brochure, "Now this is something that our customers can definitely not afford to do! As for the hair on our hair systems, you may actually find it quite difficult to tear it out of our more durable models." The site goes on to explain that "Trichotillomania is actually the name of the mental disorder where people have the uncontrollable desire to pull their own hair out.[177]

The expression, of course, means to behave frantically, to be highly frustrated, to be at wits' end. And oh, the things that put people in this hair-tearing rage.

"The anti-choice movement has me tearing my hair out in rage right now." We're not even going to cite the source because it's just a lot of estrogen rage about some Christians and others who oppose tearing babies out of their mothers' wombs at the rate of a little under a million per year. Figures are down since a high in 1995.

Jacqueline Bussie tells us in her book that she thinks Facebook ought to be called Fakebook because so many people create images of their lives there that are artificial—mostly because of what they leave out. She says, "I chose *not* to post pictures of myself arguing with my husband, puking into the

---

[177]From Lord Hair, "Hair Systems, Hair Colors and Hair Idioms," 7 Dec 2017, (https://www.lordhair.com/blog/hair-systems-and-hair-idioms)

toilet with stomach flu, tearing my hair out over office politics, or scrubbing [excrement] from my basement floor when the old sewage pipe backed up—again![178]

A mechanic posted a video of an engine running and badly misfiring at 2400 rpm. "Misfiring issue has got me tearing my hair out!" he said. Maybe the hair got in the intake? Just a thought.[179]

In the first of a two-part series about raising puppies, Melodie Davis writes in her 6 Nov 2014 column, "Another Way, "I was tearing my hair out. Yes, she had accidents, but more than that, I couldn't get the hang of what a puppy's schedule should look like." She should have gotten cats.

Back to the actual, psychological problem, there's Lindsay Thomson, who quips, "My disorder, trichotillomania, involves compulsive hair pulling. While other people may joke about 'tearing their hair out' when they are stressed, it's an everyday reality of life for me."[180]

---

[178]Jaqueline A. Bussie, *Love Without Limits*, (Minneapolis, Fortress Press, 2018) 113.

[179]George Bryant, 5 Oct 2007 (https://forums.hybridz.org/topic/60125-misfiring-issue-has-got-me-tearing-my-hair-out-video/)

[180](http://www.studentnewspaper.org/trichotillomania-i-am-literally-tearing-my-hair-out)

Tender mercies

Besides being the title of a 1983 film starring Robert Duvall, "tender mercies" is a phrase often used with irony to suggest that someone will not likely treat someone else well.

Psalm 51:1 "Have mercy upon me, O God, according to thy lovingkindness: according unto the multitude of thy tender mercies blot out my transgressions."

"Tender mercies," in the half dozen times it appears in the Psalms, is never used in irony. Instead, it is a straightforward description of the compassion of God to those who come to him. However, in Proverbs, the phrase appears again.

Proverbs 12:10 "A righteous man regardeth the life of his beast: but the tender mercies of the wicked are cruel."

Good people treat even animals well, but bad people don't even treat other people with kindness. The modern, ironic usage of "tender mercies" comes from this verse. How like us to pick the one ironic use out of all the others and bring that one into modern English.

In describing various developments among the American Indians at the turn of the 19th to the 20th century, the report of the Commissioner of the U.S. Department of the Interior said: "The Federal Government is annually expending vast sums in an effort to educate the youth of this people [Indians], only to return them in a few short years to the tender mercies of the Indian agent, whom they have been taught by their bonded school superintendents to despise" (*Annual Reports of the Department of the Interior for the Fiscal Year Ended June 30, 1903*, 231). Irony noted.

In the author's home state, a turn-of-the-century description of a typical cotton mill village gave a picture of life for a mill worker's family: "The parents in most cases work in the mills with all their children who are not excluded by the recent child labor law, and the remaining children, from twelve years downward, usually from three to six in each family, are left to the tender mercies of each other or possibly to the mother, who has all that she can do in the cooking and necessary patching..." *Reports and Resolutions of South Carolina to the General Assembly, Volume 1,* 1906, 267-268.

From President Bill Clinton's first term comes this comment: "On his first trip to Europe, President Clinton is meeting separately with Chancellor Helmut Kohl ...Together, the two leaders will search for the proper balance to reassure the Russians that they will not be ostracized, reassure the Poles that they will not be left to the tender mercies of the Russians, and help find and strengthen any Ukrainian reformers."[181]

Clearly, the tender mercies of most people are not in the least representative of those of God.

---

[181]Elizabeth Pond, "The Best of Friends," in *The Baltimore Sun,* 7 Jan 1994

Tenderhearted

This gentle term was more common a century ago, when it was used more often to describe young boys than either older ones or the feminine gender of any age—perhaps because it was remarkable, if only in a minor way, to find a boy who wasn't "rough and tumble" through and through.

Ephesians 4:32 "Be ye kind one to another, tenderhearted, forgiving one another, even as God for Christ's sake hath forgiven you."

Paul wanted every Christian to be tenderhearted. The English word translates a Greek one meaning compassionate. It is certainly possible to be compassionate without being super-sentimental, but tenderhearted often has the implication of being overly emotional, excessively sensitive. In other words, it isn't always a thoroughgoing compliment. Even when it is, it's often spoken as praise with caveat.

"Kate," on "My Kind of Parenting," writes, "My son loves fiercely. At 6, he loves playing basketball, dressing up as a superhero and building Lego creations. But he really loves cuddling with his momma and making sure his little sister is OK. …what scares me about having a tender-hearted child… isn't that he won't be capable of taking on the world; it is that the world is a cruel place."

A comment left on the Travelocity site said a restaurant's "suckling pig in traditional style" was "pretty good" …"but not for the tenderhearted." The pig was served "au naturel"… "which made my daughter a bit squeamish." The terms are not strictly synonymous.[182]

---

[182](https://www.tripadvisor.com/ShowUserReviews-g194870-d1808
566-r279782384-Su_Furriadroxu-Pula_Province_of_Cagliari_Sardinia.html#)

They know not what they do

Texas prisoner Joseph Garcia was executed on 6 Dec 2018. In 1996 he had been convicted for murdering a man in San Antonio. While in prison for that, he and six other men escaped, stole weapons, robbed a store, killed a policeman, fled to Colorado, were captured, were tried, and were convicted of murder. Garcia's attorney argued he wasn't with the group when the murder of the policeman took place, but Texas has a "Law of Parties," like the "felony murder" law in most other states, which basically says "the hand of one is the hand of all." Asked if he had any last words before being put to death, Garcia said, "Yes Sir. Dear Heavenly Father please forgive them for they know not what they do."[183]

We don't think Jesus was talking about something like this when he, the sinless Son of God, being executed for no just cause, pled the case of the soldiers who were nailing him to the cross.

Luke 23:34 "Then said Jesus, Father, forgive them; for they know not what they do."

The soldiers truly had no idea of the enormity of their sin and that of everyone responsible for that awful hour. They were blind to the fact that Jesus was the Incarnate Word of God. Unlike Garcia, who deserved his sentence, Jesus did not. Perhaps the only exception among the Roman soldiers at the site of the cross was a centurion who gazed up at Jesus and said, "Certainly, this was a righteous man."[184]

The expression, "They know not what they do," with or

---

[183]Marlane Rodriguez, "Please Forgive Them..." 6 Dec 2018 (https://www.kveo.com/news/local-news/please-forgive-them-for-they-know-not-what-they-do-texas-executed-mans-last-words/1643732367) Accessed 19 Jan 2019.

[184]Luke 23:47. Matthew 27:54 and Mark 15:39 both say the centurion said Jesus was the Son of God.

without "Forgive them," is sometimes used self-righteously, but usually with the serious attitude of someone who believes he understands vital issues that his opponents don't.

At this writing, the UK government is struggling over how, or even whether, to leave the European Union. In 2016, Frank Schell, in *The Spectator*, wrote about Britons' "shocking repudiation of their own political establishment" in voting to leave the European Union. The shocked Schell said, "The Brexit vote is non-binding and subject to a potential act of Parliament, which is sovereign. Let us hope that the MPs will see the folly of this monstrous course adopted by a small majority and forgive them for their ill-informed thinking."[185] Apparently, Mr. Schell, the "small majority" didn't think it was in Britain's best interest to stay in the EU, and doesn't want to be forgiven, but rather to have its directive followed.

Michael J. Smajda, a reader of PennLive, wrote a letter to the editor suggesting that the the modern educational system in the U.S. is turning out "the anarchists of tomorrow," who are "unwary foot soldiers who believe this country is a cesspool of inhumanity. They work tirelessly to change its constitutional concept." Warning PennLive readers of this folly, Smajda concludes, "Forgive them for they know not what they do."[186] We take issue with Smajda. We agree with him that education today is turning out many good little socialists, and we agree that they aren't aware of the evil consequences of their actions, but we don't think they should be forgiven, except in the spiritual sense. They should be defeated. Soundly. And not allowed to rise again.

---

[185]Frank Schell, "Minister, Forgive Them, For They Know Not What They Do," 27 June 2016 (https://spectator.org/minister-forgive-them-for-they-know-not-what-they-do)
[186]https://www.pennlive.com/opinion/2018/07/change_in_the_generations_penn.html

Thief in the night

Like so many other expressions from the Bible, this one winds up in titles of books, television episodes, movies and songs, and usually refers to actual thieves. Hollywood likes a good cop and robber show.

1 Thessalonians 5:2 "For yourselves know perfectly that the day of the Lord so cometh as a thief in the night."

Some users of the expression take it to mean slipping in without notice. "Like a thief in the night," said the BBC, "[Roberto] Di Matteo took temporary charge at Chelsea [Football Club, based in London] after the man who had hired him as his assistant coach…was sacked in February 2012."[187] Di Matteo came in with no fanfare, like thieves.

Paul, of course, meant that the event of Christ's return would surprise the world. Jesus had taught: "If the goodman of the house had known what hour the thief would come, he would have watched, and not have suffered his house to be broken through. Be ye therefore ready also: for the Son of man cometh at an hour when ye think not" (Luke 12:39-40). And both Jesus and Paul described the Second Coming as anything but unnoticeable. Jesus will be seen from east to west, will come with a shout, the voice of the archangel and the trump of God. "Thief in the night" means *surprise!*

When the expression is divorced from its context, however, the simple meaning of stealth persists. In 1984 in a rally speech in Atlanta, President Ronald Reagan said: "Inflation…has come like a thief in the night to rob our savings, rob our earnings, and take the bread off our tables."

---

[187] (https://www.bbc.co.uk/newsround/46864844)

Thorn in the flesh

One of the mysteries of the Bible is what constituted the Apostle Paul's "thorn in the flesh."

2 Corinthians 12:7 "And lest I should be exalted above measure through the abundance of the revelations, there was given to me a thorn in the flesh, the messenger of Satan to buffet me, lest I should be exalted above measure."

The bottom line is that we don't know what the thorn was. We only know that (1) it came from God, and (2) it came from Satan. The apparent contradiction is solved by remembering that God must allow Satan any access he has to any human being, and Satan, as smart as he is, may not have figured out that God intends to turn it against him and use it to keep his servants humble, and thus usable.

Not everyone "gets" that. Anyway, here are some self-diagnosed identifications from people you probably don't know.

"My thorn in the flesh is post traumatic stress disorder (PTSD)." – Bobby D. Gayton

"My thorn in the flesh is my relationship with food." – Donald Miller

"My thorn in the flesh is constantly wishing that one of my tweets would go viral." – Jackson Dame

"My life companion, my thorn in the flesh, is the worst, — and yet is the best!" – William Channing Gannett

"My thorn in the flesh is no' dead yet."
– Samuel Rutherford Crockett

"My thorn in the flesh—is it my husband or my alcoholism?"
– Anonymous

"My thorn in the flesh is depression and anxiety."
– Mark McNees

"My thorn in the flesh is just that—my ample flesh."
– Donya M. Dunlap

"My thorn in the flesh is dyslexia." – Jesse McGuire

"My thorn in the flesh is back pain." – Greg Anonymous

"I know what my thorn in the flesh is. And it's a daily
struggle to stay on the straight and narrow."
– "Shmuley" (See: Strait and narrow)

"My thorn in the flesh is a struggle I cannot win without
help from God, family, friends, professionals, and
medication."– Jesse Anonymous

"My thorn in the flesh is my three year old screaming
banshee of a nephew, Joriel."– Dave DeWall

"My thorn in the flesh is ME." – Bert Cobb

"Every heart knows its own trouble. You know what your
thorn in the flesh is, though you may never have told any
one, any more than Paul did." – Theophilus Stork

Through a glass darkly

English speakers familiar with the writings of Paul sometimes quote this expression from his letter to the Corinthian church:

1 Corinthians 13:12 "For now we see through a glass, darkly; but then face to face."

Paul's "glass" was either a looking glass—a mirror—or the imperfect glass of the period, which had not been in existence long. Polished metal surfaces used as mirrors would have given somewhat fuzzy and indistinct images, and imperfect glass was liable to distortion and diffusion. So, "darkly" communicates the idea of something lacking in clarity or precision. To see through a glass darkly means to fail to be able to perceive accurately, clearly and with full understanding.

Leslie Childs, editorialist with the Cumberland News in Amherst, Nova Scotia, says of her town, "The population remains just under 10,000, industries have disappeared, and, until recently many people have seen the future through a "glass darkly." Childs used the term to mean "with bleak expectations."[188]

Elizabeth Broadbent used the term for comedic effect: "My grandmother is rolling in her grave because I've lived in this [her deceased grandmother's] house for seven years and never washed the windows. Sure, I've wiped some spots here and there. But they've never seen the business end of a Windex bottle. We see as through a glass darkly in our house."[189]

---

[188]Leslie Childs, "In Amherst, everything old is new again," 18 Jan 2019 (https://www. cumberlandnewsnow.com/opinion/in-amherst-everything-old-is-new-again-276918/)

[189]Elizabeth Broadbent, "8 Household Chores I'll Never Do — Because Who Has Time For This?" (https://www.scarymommy.com/we-dont-do-chores/) Accessed 19 Jan 2019.

To everything there is a season

Almost everyone has heard the hit song, "Turn, turn, turn," by Pete Seeger, made famous by The Byrds in 1965. It can get stuck in your head. It's based on Ecclesiastes 3:1-8, and its first words are the memorable wisdom of Solomon.

Ecclesiastes 3:1 "To every thing there is a season, and a time to every purpose under the heaven."

Solomon observed that like the four seasons (not the rock and pop band!) everything else in life seemed to have an appropriate time, if it were something appropriate in the first place. In applying this wisdom, it's wise to discern whether it's time for something you're thinking of doing.

Modern use of the expression runs the gamut. In researching this saying we thought of a famous scene from *Roxanne!* the film starring Steve Martin. In one scene, Charlie (Martin) is in a restaurant-bar filled with townspeople, and a bully insults him by calling him "big nose"—Steve's prosthetic nose was about three inches long. Charlie asks the bully if that were the best he could come up with, and the bully challenges him to do better. Charlie invites the crowd to get involved. They cheer him on as he comes up with twenty "somethings better," each preceded by a subject. We won't list twenty, but here are a few ways people quote Solomon to fit their own agenda:

Marketing:" To everything there is a season...In classic scientific marketing we always understood the importance of timing. Yet we based our decisions on generalities...but now timing optimization is an exacting science."[190] There's a sinister reason many of us can't help but buy things.!

---

[190]https://www.dmnews.com/channel-marketing/social/article/13037342/timeless-truth-5-to-everything-there-is-a-season

Mundane: "'To everything there is a season, and a time to every purpose under heaven.' Super sad to report that Musgrove Plantation had to cancel our yoga event."[191] I'll bet that had them in contortions.

Scientific: "To everything there is a season: hospitalizations in Ontario demonstrate strong evidence of seasonality and predictability."[192] And it's other than Spring Fever, apparently.

Financial: "To Everything There is a Season – Except Tax Scams."[193] The key is to never click on anything that seems too good to be true or too bad to be true, and never to take calls from anyone you don't know. And learn how to say "No." And to hang up.

Construction: "Indeed, to everything there is a season, but when it comes to commercial construction, any season will do, depending on your goals, your budget and your time line."[194]

Economics: "To everything there is a season: Carbon pricing, research subsidies, and the transition to fossil-free energy." No thanks.[195]

Fashion: "To everything there is a season except fashion these days...It used to be that retailers and designers dictated what went into stores for each of the six seasons of womenswear (menswear had two), and therefore what we would wear when...but things began to change about a decade ago with the advent of transition seasons...they created a monster."[196] The author wears the same clothes all

---

[191]https://www.facebook.com/TheClubSSI/photos/to-everything-there-is-a-season-and-a-time-to-every-purpose-under-heaven-super-s/10155594378995918/

[192]From the Institute for Clinical Evaluative Sciences.

[193]Raskob Kambourian Financial Advisors

[194] https://www.dbsg.com/blog/when-it-comes-to-commercial-construction-to-everything-there-is-a-season

[195] https://www.journals.uchicago.edu/doi/abs/10.1086/701805?mobileUi=0&

[196] Kiral Schlecter, https://www.readingeagle.com/life/article/to-everything-there-is-a-season-except-for-fashion

year long. Too little closet for any other strategy.

Musical: "Symphony of the Hills - Music for All Time - To Everything There is a Season (Purchase tickets >Here<)"[197]

Investing: "To Everything There Is A Season—Instead of ignoring the seasonality of economies and financial markets, embrace it! Bias toward growth assets when the economy is growing and avoid them when it is not."[198] We pay other people to think like this—it's like talking in Swahili to us.

Etiquette: "To Everything, There Is a Season. Time to start the social season. Gentlemen, please remove your baseball caps. Ladies, please remove your, ah, baseball caps."[199] The author heartily agrees. We don't know why it's bad manners, for instance, to wear a hat in a restaurant; it just is. So there.

Educational: "You've likely heard the old saying, 'to everything there is a season.' This timeless wisdom applies to many aspects of life—including, yes, benchmark assessments." The writer of the previous sentence is an educator. Old saying? Why can't teachers, educators, *schools* just say something came from the Bible? Would that be so bad?

Philosophical: "Turning the paper to the obituaries my gaze froze and then widened on a familiar face to me and at the Oak Grill. My eyes shuttled a couple of times back and forth between the paper and the empty stool at the end of the counter...To everything there is a season."[200]

197
https://www.kerrvilletexascvb.com/events/2019/symphony-of-the-hills---music-for-all-time---to-everything-there-is-a-season

198 http://www.calyxadvisors.com/blog/to_everything_there_is_a_season

199 https://www.washingtonpost.com/archive/lifestyle/2004/08/29/to-everything-there-is-a-season/fc6430fc-84f2-4f2b-80da-61c4883df788/?utm_term=.4ba77deef7e0

200 https://www.austindailyherald.com/2011/06/urlick-to-everything-there-is-a-season/

Turn the other cheek

Matthew 5:39 "But I say unto you, That ye resist not evil: but whosoever shall smite thee on thy right cheek, turn to him the other also."

The expression, "Turn the other cheek," has resulted in many a debate between Christians and non-Christians, and even among Christians themselves, about how far Jesus meant us to go. Our opinion, just generally, is that he meant it: for interpersonal relationships; especially regarding insults; where witness to godly character is important; not for situations of actual violence to oneself or others; and not as a rule for government at all.

Most of the time when people say it, they're referencing the teaching of Jesus.

"But I say unto you, That ye resist not evil: but whosoever shall smite thee on thy right cheek, turn to him the other also…Our laws are fairly accepting when it comes to the use of violence in cases of self-defense. Things are less clear when it comes to defending yourself against officers of the law."[201]

"Rare is the man who takes no umbrage when being assailed unjustly, who feels no anger when his most-cherished beliefs are attacked and his name besmirched. That said, how is one to move beyond this feeling of defensiveness? How does one decide when to 'turn the other cheek' and when it is 'a time to speak'? This is a matter of prudential judgment, I think, so there can be no hard-and-fast rule, no mathematical formula into which one stuffs data and out of which is spit an infallible answer."[202]

Well said, we think.

---

[201]http://think.kera.org/2019/01/17/what-happens-if-we-dont-turn-the-other-cheek/
[202]Karl Keeting, "When Not to Turn the Other Cheek" *Catholic Answers*, 1 Jan 1997.

Two are better than one

A simple expression already in the language, the King James Version memorialized it.

Ecclesiastes 4:9-11 "Two are better than one; because they have a good reward for their labour."

Solomon also said that if they fall, one will lift the other up, and if two sleep together, they keep each other warm.

"Two are better than one: infant language learning from video improves in the presence of peers," say researchers.[203] We guess as long as children are going to be staring at screens from the moment they come out of the womb, they might as well be doing it in pairs, to get the most out of it.

"Two are better than one. If you are considering getting a cat why not get a pair. With two cats you get twice the personality and double the fun."[204] So says the St. Helens Adoption Center. Well, we say, make them BOGO. Seriously, the author and wife have had pairs twice and they *are* more fun.

Somebody asked English experts, "'Two are better than one' or 'Two is better than one?' Which is correct?" Unless you're talking about numerals, it's "are." Two cats *are*.

"If two are better than one, three are better than two," says Chaim Locker, M.D., to the question of whether "a third arterial conduit to the right coronary circulation improve[s] survival."[205] It's a pressing issue for heart bypass surgeons. Further, go back to Ecclesiastes, after the verses we've already quoted: "and a threefold cord is not quickly broken." Case closed.

---

[203]https://www.pnas.org/content/115/40/9859/tab-figures-data
[204]https://www.cats.org.uk/sthelens/adopt-a-cat/two-are-better-than-one
[205]https://www.jtcvs.org/article/S0022-5223(17)32327-9/fulltext

Two-edged sword

Hebrews 4:12 "For the word of God is quick, and powerful, and sharper than any twoedged sword."

Something that cuts going either direction is either double the danger or double the success, a benefit and a liability.

The world of medicine seems to be rife with these dangerous weapons:

The National Institutes of Health suggests that melanin (your skin pigment) is a two-edged sword.[206] On the one hand, the more you have of it, the less likely you are to come down with skin cancer. On the other hand, the more of it you have, the more likely you are to have damaging oxygen species. (Whatever those are.) Tanned if you do, tanned if you don't. (Actually, "darker" here means by natural complexion, not sunbathing. We just couldn't resist the pun.)

Research Gate says fluoride is "a two-edged sword. Ingestion of large amounts is associated with fluorosis and other ailments; while inadequate amounts associated with dental caries."[207]

And the American Journal of Respiratory and Critical Care Medicine says that "Inhaled corticosteroids in chronic obstructive pulmonary disease" are "a two-edged sword."[208] Corticosteroids help treat COPD, but in doing so, they increase the risk of pneumonia.

In an article titled, "Vaccines – A Two-Edged Sword," author Nirupama Shankar gives anecdotal evidence of a child successfully vaccinated against childhood diseases and another child who developed autism as a result of vaccination—in a case where the link was confirmed. Shankar said some vaccines

---

[206]https://www.ncbi.nlm.nih.gov/pubmed/9266603
[207]https://www.researchgate.net/publication/270879591_Fluoride_A_Two-edged_Sword
[208]https://www.atsjournals.org/doi/abs/10.1164/rccm.201605-0942ED

have stuff like formaldehyde, mercury, methanol, and antifreeze in them, but he advised people to make their own decisions. The author isn't jumping on any bandwagon. Shankar's article was published with a nice picture of a sword to illustrate his title, but it was a one-edged saber. Maybe he couldn't find a two-edged sword picture. Anyway, he's not an M.D. or a Ph.D., not a scientist of any kind. Our belief is that vaccination is still the best bet against diseases that can leave you deaf, paralyzed, or kill you, and the risks you run by not being vaccinated are higher than if you are. Use Shankar's own analogy: If you don't get vaccinated, you "cut" your risk of autism from a vaccination to zero. But you cut your immunity to zero, too, leaving you vulnerable to all the terrible results of childhood diseases. Okay, it's a crapshoot, but we'll bet on responsible vaccination over returning to the old days.

A blogger named "Revere," on Science Blogs, had the temerity to suggest that piped water is a two-edged sword. Revere said piped water supplies (which began in earnest just before the Civil War) dramatically reduced waterborne infectious diseases like typhoid and trickled down to helping prevent pneumonia. But the piping itself made distribution of poisons easier as well. He gave the illustration of a Colorado town recently poisoned en masse by salmonella, coming from the municipal water system, which draws from deep wells.[209]

Enough of medicine. As to digital technology, IEEE says, "technology—a two-edged sword," and references its own code of ethics, which remind their professionals of digital technology's "appropriate application, *and* potential consequences." They advise everybody to "dull one side of the sword."[210] Now there's some simple advice we can applaud.

---

[209]https://scienceblogs.com/effectmeasure/2008/03/24/piped-water-two-edged-sword
[210]https://ieeexplore.ieee.org/document/8307798

Under my wing [or his, etc.]

Matthew 23:37 "O Jerusalem, Jerusalem, thou that killest the prophets, and stonest them which are sent unto thee, how often would I have gathered thy children together, even as a hen gathereth her chickens under her wings, and ye would not!"

The expression means to take care of, and often it includes the concept of training in special skills or secrets of a business.

One of Jason Ross's characters says, "Vincent…I am offering to take you under my wing and teach you everything that you need to know not only about this business but also how to survive in this business."[211] This author felt that way a lifetime ago, but in his case there was no bigger bird, no wings to be under. It was fly or fall, and too often he plummeted.

Corey Davis of the Tennessee Titans in 2018 said of receiver Harry Douglas, "Harry helped me not only in football, but life, family, and how to handle things…I was a rookie, and didn't really know much. So he took me under his wing and helped me out a lot." It must have helped. Davis had 65 receptions for 891 yards, averaging 13.7 yards per catch.[212]

And actress Liv Tyler wrote a tribute to the late Bernardo Bertolucci, crediting him with invaluable lessons on acting: "The little secrets of how to capture the magic. He took me under his wing and let me fly."[213] We're not sure how that works, being under the wing and still flying. Mixed metaphors. But when credit is due to someone, give it, and she gave touching praise.

---

[211]Jason Ross, *Don't Wound What You Can't Kill* (Xlibris Corp, 2010) 21.
[212](https://titanswire.usatoday.com/2019/01/07/corey-davis-says-former-titans-receiver-harry-douglas-took-him-under-his-wing/)
[213](http://www.oystermag.com/2018/11/liv-tyler-pens-beautiful-tribute-to-the-late-bernardo-bertolucci/)

Vengeance is mine

Romans 12:19 "Vengeance is mine; I will repay, saith the Lord."

Kathryn Reklis wrote a review of *Django Unchained,* the 2012 Quentin Tarantino film. Near the end, "a freed slave named Django rides across a Mississippi plain, planning to wreak vengeance on the plantation owners holding his wife captive...Salvific undertones are made explicit in the pulsating rhythms and lyrics of the accompanying song by John Legend: 'I'm not afraid to do the Lord's work / You say vengeance is his, but I'm gonna do it first.'"[214]

What does the principle of vengeance being God's mean for man's redress of wrongs? It's a complicated issue, of course; not all forms of justice amount to vengeance. As with "turn the other cheek" (q.v.), it is a matter of "prudential judgment."

Without question, however, final judgment is God's, and no one in this life need think that if he doesn't exact justice for some great evil, no one ever will. That's one of the direct applications of Paul's statement—which, by the way, is a quotation of Deuteronomy 35:32.

The entertainment and publishing industries being what they are, however, most films, television episodes and books that draw on this familiar phrase as titles for their drama tell stories where people are anything but willing to defer to God to exact vengeance. As a case in point, Bill Neal's book, *Vengeance Is Mine,* recounts the real-life, scandalous love triangle of 1912 in Texas that sparked an eighty-year feud. The publisher describes it as "saga of passion, violence, and revenge, of retribution but never redemption." That's the problem with human payback: it does not deeply satisfy.

---

[214]https://www.christiancentury.org/article/2013-01/vengeance-mine

Wages of sin

Few scriptures are more lampooned or denigrated by critics
and enemies of Christianity than this core teaching of the New
Testament, which comes from Paul's pen.

**Romans 6:23 "For the wages of sin is death; but the gift
of God is eternal life through Jesus Christ our Lord."**

Often used without, "is death," the expression is often
employed in accusations about somebody *else's* sins:
"She had tramped the streets for weeks on her weary
errand, and the only living wages that were offered her were
the wages of sin."[215] The reference is, of course, to prostitution.
"Many hospitals, even into the 20th century, refused to admit
those whose complaints were the wages of sin, and many
physicians would not treat them."[216] Another, only barely
oblique, reference to prostitution or simply illicit sex.
"Shortly before I arrived in Eastbourne for the Christmas
holidays, my chin broke out in a spotty rash and my toenails
became infected with an unsightly fungus. Clearly these were
psychosomatic responses to stress. But at the time I was
convinced that they were the wages of sin, retribution for my
betrayal of Sheba."[217] More about sexual sin, this time self-
remonstrance. (But how is a fungus psychosomatic?)
"The discovery of penicillin decreased the cost of syphilis
and thereby played an important role in shaping modern
sexuality." So says the author's description of his article on that
subject.[218] Penicillin was discovered in 1928 by Alexander

---

[215]Jacob August Riis, *How the Other Half Lives: Studies Among the Tenements of New York*
(New York, Penguin Books, 1997) 176.

[216]E. E. Shelp, *Sexuality and Medicine: Volume II: Ethical Viewpoints in Transition* (Berlin,
Springer Science and Business Media, 2012) 81.

[217]Zoë Heller, *Notes on a Scandal: What Was She Thinking?* (London, Picador, 2006)

[218]A. M. Francis, "The wages of sin: how the discovery of penicillin reshaped modern
sexuality" (Archives of Sexual Behavior, January 2013)

Fleming. It wasn't until 1943 that medical scientists realized penicillin successfully treated syphilis. When they did, this "wages-of-sin" disease "collapsed" (in statistical terms) and the modern sexual revolution took off.

Sins other than sex have been indicted for paying painful wages: "Judging by newspaper headlines of the early 1930s, popular wisdom viewed economics through a biblical lens: recessions were the wages of sin"[219]—for living too high on the hog during an economic boom.

Students of the economy debunked the religious theory that economic downturn should be blamed on sin: "The Depression mocked the Puritan assumption that failure in life was the wages of sin when even the hardest-working, most pious husbands began to lose hope."[220] Even so, other cultural sins were at fault.

Gambling, too, has been a target: "If these were the wages of sin, they stood doubly condemned in being derived from online gambling," wrote Jeremy Warner, typifying the condemnation by British liberals of an online betting firm's paycheck to its founder, Denise Coates, of £265 million. Warner thought she should be celebrated.[221]

Many of the things called the wages of sin are connected with fornication, drinking, smoking, and gambling—the "big four," in some religious contexts. But "sin" in the verse in Romans, is about the overall spiritual infection, not merely one of its symptomatic practices. And death is spiritual and final.

---

[219]Sylvia Nassar, in Robert Samuelson, "Causes of the Crisis" (Real Clear Politics, 19 Mar 2012).

[220]Walter McDougall, *Promised Land, Crusader State: The American Encounter with the World Since 1776* (Boston, Houghton Mifflin Harcourt, 1997) 148.

[221](https://www.telegraph.co.uk/business/2018/11/24/betting-boss-should-celebrated-not-vilified-265m-payday/)

Wallowing in the mire

This expression was an indictment of claimants to Christian faith who returned to non-Christian living.

2 Peter 2:22 "The dog is turned to his own vomit again; and the sow that was washed to her wallowing in the mire."

The phrase is rarely used popularly in its original context. "Draining the swamp or wallowing in the mire?" began Eugene Robinson, in a piece excoriating President Donald Trump. Robinson continued, "It is our duty to demand ethical integrity from our presidents, and Donald Trump cannot be allowed to make himself an exception."[222] Well, perspective is important.

"As for the issue of illegal immigration, the Left is wallowing in the mire of hypocrisy like a pig in mud-slinging,"[223] says "Redstate" of (chiefly) Democrat condemnation of (chiefly) Republicans and President Trump of attempts to build a wall on the southern border of the U.S.

"Wallowing in the mire that is FedEx Ground," said one employee of FedEx in an anonymous review of the shipping giant.[224] Sounds like mudslinging to us.

Mike Kiley, a sports writer for the *Chicago Tribune,* says the Edmonton Oilers "are not only the National Hockey League's most ineffective offense, but are wallowing in the mire of a 2-9-2 start, their worst."[225]

---

[222](http://www.lowellsun.com/opinion/ci_30598529/eugene-robinson-draining-swamp-or-wallowing-mire)
[223](https://www.countable.us/articles/18281-obama-sides-trump-racist-immigration-position)
[224](https://www.glassdoor.com/Reviews/Employee-Review-FedEx-Ground-RVW15720507.htm)
[225](https://www.chicagotribune.com/news/ct-xpm-1990-11-08-9004040437-story.html)

Wandering stars

Not many people use this expression except astronomers. But it's picturesque and evocative of the mysteries of space.

Jude 1:13 "Raging waves of the sea, foaming out their own shame; wandering stars, to whom is reserved the blackness of darkness for ever."

Jude's description was of non-Christian people who worm their way into churches in an insidious and sinister attempt to corrupt them. But the phrase probably predated Jude, a description of heavenly phenomena that defied human explanation.

George H. A. Cole references "ancient times when the five planets that can be seen from Earth without a telescope were called the 'wandering stars.'"[226] Astronomer Mike Lynch says, "Back in the day, folks didn't know about any of this and saw the planets as wandering stars. In fact, they really didn't know what stars were, period."[227] Apparently it's not only planets that "wander." Indeed, astronomer David Salisbury says, "A new map of the Milky Way, created by scientists with the Sloan Digital Sky Survey (SDSS), shows that a surprisingly large proportion, 30 percent, of its stars are wanderers that have dramatically changed orbits during their lifetimes."[228]

Illustratively, Sholem Aleichem, writing in the mid 19th century, said of a young artist, "He will not be here for long, *meine Damen und Herren,* but sadly only for a short time, like all great wandering stars that vanish as quickly as they appear."[229]

---

[226] (https://www.worldscientific.com/worldscibooks/10.1142/p333)

[227] (https://www.futurity.org/milky-way-stars-galaxies-974992/)

[228] (https://www.postbulletin.com/life/lifestyles/starwatch-the-case-of-the-wandering-stars/article_eace76df-25f1-5c0d-9b05-438c8b6426b6.html)

[229] Sholem Aleichem, *Wandering Stars* (New York, Penguin Books, 2009) 129.

Wash your hands of the matter

Pontius Pilate made himself famous not only for delivering Jesus to be crucified, but also for using a visual idiom of his day to pretend to be guiltless when he did.

Matthew 27:24 "When Pilate saw that he could prevail nothing, but that rather a tumult was made, he took water, and washed his hands before the multitude, saying, I am innocent of the blood of this just person: see ye to it."

Today's usage of the expression sometimes has the original sense:

To a question of what to do about a certain region's "lack of water closets" (bathrooms, for those not in the UK), one responder said, "I suggest you wash your hands of the matter by closing what facilities there are, and allow citizens to get back to basics by making it legal for any of us to use the nearest bush."[230] But what about women?

Other situations find the expression used to indicate legitimate avoidance of guilt:

Australian interviewer Kerry O'Brien spoke with Prime Minister Howard John in 2000, about mandatory sentencing laws, and brought up the case of the dramatic difference of the treatment of a 17-year old as opposed to one who is 18. O'Brien apparently thought giving juveniles a relative pass and then suddenly treating people differently after their 18th birthdays was wrong in principle. He asked, "On the basis of what you are saying, you wash your hands of the matter if an 18 year old, a 19 year old or a 20 year old...ends up in prison for stealing biscuits or textas or paint or something of that ilk."

The Prime Minister responded, in part, "You have to draw

---

[230](https://nsindex.net/wiki/NationStates_Issue_No._525)

the line somewhere. The law from time immemorial has drawn a distinction."[231] And that, as they say, was that. Hands washed and dried.

Other uses of hand washing are simply good advice as to how to settle a matter completely:

Advising their small-business readers what to do when slapped with a lawsuit, the SJS Law Firm says, "Don't just hire an attorney to handle the lawsuit and wash your hands of the matter. Stay on top of your attorney and make sure you understand the process, the status of the case, and the attorney's strategy."[232]

An Amazon.com seller wonders what to do about a complaint when the customer won't follow up with more details. Offers another seller, " I would urge you to just process the refund and wash your hands of the matter."[233] J. C. Penney invented the slogan, "The customer is always right." He may not be, but treating him as if he were usually keeps him as a customer.

Sharpe&Abel Lawyers advise employers whose workers file claims over the failure of safety products that though lawyers may be appointed to handle the case, "this does not mean that you can wash your hands of the matter…it's your reputation on the line. Take an active part in the management of a claim and don't just leave it to your insurers and lawyers."[234]

---

[231](https://pmtranscripts.pmc.gov.au/release/transcript-11457)

[232](https://www.thesjslawfirm.com/2015/05/17/when-darkness-falls-handling-the-horrors-of-small-business-ownership/)

[233](https://sellercentral.amazon.com/forums/t/return-request-needs-more-information-but-customer-is-not-replying/279332/4)

[234](https://sharpeandabel.com/articles/2013/liability-when-safety-products-fail.html)

Robert F. Simms

Weak as water

Everyone who has ever been in love knows what it means to be weak in the knees, but fear does the same thing, as the prophet Ezekiel observed and predicted.

Ezekiel 7:17 "All hands shall be feeble, and all knees shall be weak as water."

The expression today is far more common in the UK than in America. It generally is not found in the prophetic sense but as a simple description of someone who is weak or something, such as an argument, that is insubstantial.

A reader criticized the theory of an article in the *Queensland Times* (AU) that attempted to attribute a surge in boat buying from Indonesia to smugglers. The reader found the argument "weak as water," and suggested another reason, which served as an indictment of the Australian government.[235]

Triple M, an Aussie news outlet, quoted Andrew Jarman on a teapot tempest in the soccer world: "'The AFL - in terms of the match review panel being weak as water not suspending people for jumper punches,'" said Triple M. The author is lost whenever people discuss soccer.

For a rarer U.S. use of the term, Carter Wren, on "Talking about Politics," left a short entry in 2015 critiquing a U.S. Administration move: "Obama's sending fifty soldiers to Iraq to whip ISIS. Fifty soldiers…Weak as water's not going to whip ISIS. As they used to say back in the days when Americans fought wars to win, *It's time for Obama to get tough – or get out of the way.*"[236] The emphasis was Wren's. As of January 2016, Obama was out of the way. Time to get tough.

---

[235](https://www.qt.com.au/news/boat-buy-story-weak-as-water/2790949/)
[236](https://talkingaboutpolitics.com/weak-as-water/)

White as snow

We remember the true story of a missionary on one of those proverbially remote islands somewhere in the south Pacific, trying to communicate the gospel to the islanders. He came to Isaiah 1:18 where Isaiah preached to his nation a message of repentance. If they turned to the Lord, he said, "though your sins be as scarlet, they shall be as white as snow." The islanders had never seen snow. They had no idea what this verse meant.

The missionary struggled with whether to keep repeating the translation provided. Finally he decided that communication was paramount. The islanders had never seen snow; but they had seen chickens. "They shall be as white as chickens," was the translation.

This expression comes from both the Old and New Testaments. In addition to Isaiah, a memorable use of the term occurs in the gospels.

Mark 9:3 "And his raiment became shining, exceeding white as snow; so as no fuller on earth can white them."

This was the disciples' description of Jesus during his Transfiguration.

In addition to having described Mary's little lamb, "white as snow" has often been used to describe the complexion of a dying person, or someone who has simply been scared to death! —as an alternative to being as white as a sheet.

Hunter Alex DeVito tells about being in New Jersey and hearing of "The White Buck." Local claimants to seeing him were asked if he were really white. "He was as white as snow!"[237] Albino. Truly rare.

---

[237] (http://www.ccsindians.com/Alex%20DeVito/whitebuck.htm)

Wisdom of Solomon

Every once in a while someone will use this expression to explain his inability to come up with a perfect solution or answer. It comes from the biblical history of the kings of Israel.

1 Kings 4:34 "And there came of all people to hear the wisdom of Solomon, from all kings of the earth, which had heard of his wisdom."

The phrase appears also in the New Testament, where Jesus compared himself to Solomon.

Joe L. Blevins, in his historical book, *After the Republic,* tells a story through "Andrew," a freed slave adopted by the Cherokee following the defeat of Santa Anna in 1836. Andrew wrote in his periodic diaries, "We miss the peaceful times we had in east Texas living with the Cherokee. This war is bigger than all of us put together, and it would take the Wisdom of Solomon to figure it all out."[238] And things haven't changed much, Andrew.

San Francisco Director of Taxi Services Chris Hayashi was trying to work out a compromise on some controversial matter. An interviewer said to her, "You're talking about taxi drivers, I think I said. You put two of them together in a room and you have five opinions. It would take the wisdom of Solomon to get them to agree on anything—much less your idea."[239]

Edith Roberts, in a roundup of pending SCOTUS cases in December 2018, described the question of whether Congress had disestablished the boundaries of an Indian reservation in Oklahoma. She quoted Garrett Epps, who said, "It's tempting

---

[238]Joe Blevins, *After the Republic* (Xlibris Corporation, 2008) 128.
[239]((http://phantomcabdriverphites.blogspot.com/2014/05/chris-hayashi-wisdom-of-solomon.html)

to say that it would take the wisdom of Solomon to resolve this dispute," but that "fear—even fear of gaping prison doors—is not usually a great basis for judgment." Given how long Indian issues have defied easy solution, it would be nice to have Solomon around.

Occasionally someone will attempt to closely imitate Solomon. John Littell, in his book, *Carvel: the Christmas Cat,* describes a school Christmas pageant put on jointly by a high school and elementary school. The high school principal, Dr. Hunter, had to pick a director. Littell writes, "After much prayer and meditation, Dr. Hunter showed he had the wisdom of Solomon. ...He...cleaved The Pageant in two, giving the high school actors and sets to Miss Houghton and the elementary school actors and props to Mrs. Terry."

Dr. Hunter didn't actually imitate Solomon, however. Solomon didn't split the baby (Read 1 Kings 3:16-28). He said he was going to, only to prompt the real mother to give up her claim to the child so as to spare his life.

And Dr. Hunter's "wisdom" came back to bite him with squabbling between the directors. "Dr. H. had wanted peace on Earth, but he had unwittingly unleashed Armageddon."[240]

There seems to be decreasing competition with Solomon for wisdom these days, especially on the national leadership level. Oh, for a few founding fathers, who self-evidently had a great measure of Solomon's understanding.

---

[240]John Littell, *Carvel: the Christmas Cat* (Chicago, Sourcebooks, 2003) 161.

Woe is me

This phrase originates with Isaiah, in describing his call to the prophetic ministry.

Isaiah 6:5: "Woe *is* me! for I am undone; because I *am* a man of unclean lips, and I dwell in the midst of a people of unclean lips..."

The expression occurs also in the Psalms and Jeremiah. A word first on the grammatical form of the phrase.

Willliam Safire wrote in 1993 about the common usage of "me" instead of "I" in English constructions where the pronoun is a predicate nominative: a pronoun after a form of the verb "to be." He referred to a "breed of language lover" that preferred to say, "I am he," rather than, "I am him," and he chose "him" on the grounds that it had a long history, including Shakespeare and the Bible. Safire said, "If both Shakespeare's heroine and the biblical prophet said, 'Woe is me,' who are the predicate nominatarians to insist on 'Woe is I'?"[241]

But then Safire did some study and discovered (as I knew before he did) that the Hebrew of Isaiah 6:5 doesn't have the verb "is." Note that in the quotation of Isaiah's self-deprecating statement above, the words "is" and later "am" are in italics. In the King James and other translations, italics are used to indicate that the English translators supplied a word not in the original Hebrew (OT) or Greek (NT). The Hebrew of Isaiah's pithy admission says simply, "Woe me," or even, "woe to me." The translators supplied a verb because that made a complete sentence. And yes, in their day they allowed the use of the

---

[241]William Safire, On Language: Woe Is Not Me (New York Times Magazine, Oct 17, 1993, *The Internet*), available from *https://www.nytimes.com/1993/10/17/magazine/on-language-woe-is-not-me.html*, The Internet; accessed Dec 16, 2018.

objective case "me."

By the time of the New Testament, Paul said *"ouai moi"* (ουαι μοι), or "woe [to] me," if I preach not the gospel. The Greek was like the Hebrew in not having or requiring a preposition.

The phrase "woe is me" was more frequently "woe unto me" in times past, and it is used today in either form but probably more the former.

Its meaning is no mystery, of course. It refers to the expectation of calamity, of negative consequences, usually severe, because of present choices or events. Unfortunately for the preservation of its original, biblical sense, "Woe is me" is often said in response to trivial problems, or even used facetiously. The Urban Dictionary (*urbandictionary.com*) says that "woe is me" is "used to indicate that you've called yourself out for complaining too much."

This trivialization of the phrase is a good example of the distancing of ancient sayings from their roots, or even the reversal of their meaning, that frequently takes place in our culture. Like "sign of the times" (*q.v.*) many phrases that come from the Bible have been stripped of their original import and have become merely idioms for the mundane.

As examples:

Eminem (White rap singer): "A lot of problems I had with fame I was bringing on myself. A lot of self-loathing, a lot of woe-is-me."

Peyton Manning (Former QB with Indianapolis Colts): "I walked around for a while angry, in a bad mood—'Woe is me.' I've gotten over that. It doesn't do any good."

William Shakespeare (Do you need help, here?): "Woe is me to have seen what I have seen, see what I see."

Vincent van Gogh (He of one ear): "If I do nothing, if I study nothing, if I cease searching, then woe is me, I am lost."

Wolf in sheep's clothing

Wolf in Sheep's Clothing, believe it or not, is the name of a restaurant in Venice (California). The author has been to Venice, on one of his two motorcycle trips across the country to Los Angeles and points north. You can find just about anything in L.A., much of it bizarre. What the connection is between the name and the cuisine, we don't know.

Matthew 7:15 "Beware of false prophets, which come to you in sheep's clothing, but inwardly they are ravening wolves."

The expression, "wolf in sheep's clothing," which comes from this verse, obviously refers to someone, or some human enterprise, that purports to belong where he or she joins or associates, but is, in fact, there to subvert, to spy, or to destroy.

Ben Glass and Mark Blane, both attorneys, authored the book, *Wolf in Sheep's Clothing: What Your Insurance Company Doesn't Want You to Know.* Styled as an exposé, the book documents how insurances companies, which "are in every aspect of our lives-from birth to death,"[242] purport to guarantee you against loss, but routinely manage to evade paying for what should be fully covered claims.

Sadly, the expression has application to the original context: the church. News from Haiti in July 2018 was that "James Arbaugh was a wolf in sheep's clothing: He posed as a selfless missionary, when in reality, he was exploiting his position to prey on and sexually abuse vulnerable children in one of the most impoverished areas of the world."[243]

---

[242]Ben Glass and Mark Blane, *Wolf in Sheep's Clothing* (Celebrity Press, 2011).
[243] Brian Benczkowski, assistant U.S. attorney general, in a news release.

Writing [is] on the wall

Daniel 5:5 "In the same hour came forth fingers of a man's hand, and wrote over against the candlestick upon the plaister of the wall of the king's palace: and the king saw the part of the hand that wrote."

What was written was " Mene, mene, tekel, upharsin." The prophet Daniel interpreted for the king, Belshazzar, in verses 26-28. The king was about to be overthrown.

For someone to see the writing (or handwriting) on the wall, is to perceive that something undesirable is about to happen or that previous actions are about to have consequences.

Ida LeClair, a comedian based in Maine, wrote a blog entry on her website, Ida's Website (inventive), about computer dating. She was waxing realistic about her and her husband's mortality and said: "At our age, the writing's on the wall. There's a 50/50 chance, right? You're going to be the last one standing or you're not."[244]

Robert Graboyes writes on *InsideSources* that "digital technologies enable patients to perform diagnostic and therapeutic tasks that were once the sole preserve of doctors. Doctors, whose privileged paternalism dates from ancient Egypt, can barely see the handwriting on the wall."[245] Oh, we think they can. In fact, after people self-diagnose and get it wrong, they need even *more* treatment and medicine. Besides, doctors pretty much stopped wanting to see us for things we can figure out and treat ourselves for, when they stopped making house calls.

And then there's Redd Foxx, who quipped, "If you can see the handwriting on the wall, you're on the toilet."

---

[244](https://www.idaswebsite.com/computer-dating/)
[245](https://www.insidesources.com/health-care-summer-reading-list/)

You reap what you sow

This obvious bit of wisdom from farming became for Jesus Christ a teaching about the lives expected of God's people: Ye shall know them by their fruits. Do men gather grapes of thorns, or figs of thistles? (Matthew 7:16). In the writing of Paul to one of the churches, he rephrased it succinctly.

Galatians 6:7 "Be not deceived; God is not mocked: for whatsoever a man soweth, that shall he also reap."

We hear the truism today without the "thee's and thou's," so to speak (though there aren't any in this verse).

After the 2016 U.S. Presidential elections, Felix Fitzpatrick wrote in *Al Día*, "Hillary Clinton did not use the Latino Vote properly to ensure victory…You reap what you sow. Ms. Clinton poorly made the political bed that now we all have to lie in."[246] Fitzpatrick "might oughta" recalculate. At the end of only two years of Trump's presidency, Hispanic median income was up; home ownership was up; and employment was *way* down. Americans are liking the harvest—even those who don't like the President.

In a letter to the editor of the *Daily Citizen-News* headed, "You reap what you sow," a reader wrote, "This letter is intended for the person who hit my car on Nov. 9 (causing considerable damage), while I was parked at Hamilton Medical Center…What goes around comes around."[247] That's precisely what the expression means. We'd love to know whether the malefactor was ever appropriately rewarded for hit-and-run, and we'd like to hope that whoever stole our utility trailer will run into the same, fitting harvest.

[246]http://aldianews.com/articles/opinion/op-ed-you-reap-what-you-sow/44490)
[247]Cathi Rogers, a Letter to the Editor, *Daily Citizen-News*, Dalton, GA, 14 Nov 2016.

Your sin will find you out

An expression with religious-specific language is likely to survive mostly in the religious community. Sinners don't like to be told that they're going be discovered and face the music. We're all sinners, so we should all take the message to heart.

Numbers 32:23 "But if ye will not do so, behold, ye have sinned against the LORD: and be sure your sin will find you out."

On an Internet forum for troubling questions, a woman calling herself Blogsphere wrote that she got into a sexual relationship with her 20-year-old son. She asked the forum for advice. Of course, replies include "Stop!" and "It's of the devil." Someone called Penalty82 wrote, "Your SIN will find you out one day." From the language Blogsphere used in her tale, we think it was actually fictitious, designed to incite lust in readers. But the answer was on target. If her story is for real, we imagine she'll be found out *before* Judgment Day.

Two men in Ohio killed a "celebrity" fifteen-point buck about nine years old—a deer familiar throughout the region, named, and often seen and photographed. The deer was off limits for hunting under a new (2011) law. For some stupid reason the hunters posted pictures on the Ohio Division of Wildlife's website! That got them identified, charged and convicted, and they were ordered to make restitution of a record $13,277. The news of the conviction, posted on a deer hunting site, prompted a reader to comment, "What were these guys thinking? Be sure you sin will find you out."[248]

---

[248](https://www.deeranddeerhunting.com/articles/deer-news/brain-dead-ohio-poachers-punished)

Index of Alternate Expressions

An eye for an eye, a tooth for a tooth
    (See: Eye for eye, tooth for tooth)
Arise and shine
    (See: Rise and shine)
As you sow so shall you reap
    (See: You reap what you sow)
As a sheep to the slaughter
    (See: Led as a sheep to the slaughter)
Be sure your sin will find you out
    (See: Your sin will find you out)
Cast the first stone
    (See: Casting the first stone)
Cast your bread upon the waters
    (See: Bread upon the waters)
Charity shall cover a multitude of sins
    (See: Love covers a multitude of sins)
Cup runneth over
    (See: My cup runneth over)
Don't cast your pearls before swine
    (See: Casting your pearls before swine)
Dust to dust
    (See: Ashes to ashes, dust to dust)
Father, forgive them, for they know not what they do
    (See: They know not what they do)
For everything there is a season
    (See: To everything there is a season)
Forgive them, for they know not what they do
    (See: They know not what they do)
From strength to strength
    (See: Strength to strength)
Fruits of your loins
    (See: Fruit of his loins)
Get your house in order

(See: Put your house in order)
Gird your loins
(See: Gird up your loins)
Handwriting on the wall
(See: Writing on the wall)
Hellfire and brimstone
(See: Fire and brimstone)
In a moment of time
(See: Moment of time)
Lamb to the slaughter
(See: Led as a sheep to the slaughter)
Left hand know what thy right hand doeth
(See: Don't let your left hand know, etc.)
Leopard [change] his spots
(See: Can a leopard change his spots?)
Let him who is without sin cast the first stone
(See: Casting the first stone)
Let not the sun go down on your wrath
(See: Don't go to bed angry)
Lick the dust
(See: Bite the dust)
Like a sheep to slaughter
(See: Led as a sheep to the slaughter)
Living off the fat of the land
(See: Fat of the land)
Money is the root of all evil
(See: Love of money is the root of all evil)
My brother's keeper
(See: Brother's keeper)
My cross to bear
(See: Cross to bear)
No room for them in the inn
(See: No room in the inn)
Pearls before swine
(See: Casting your pearls before swine)

Person is known by the company he keeps
  (See: Known by the company he keeps)
Reap what you sow
  (See: You reap what you sow)
Root of all evil
  (See: Love of money is the root of all evil)
Set your house in order
  (See: Put your house in order)
Set your teeth on edge
  (See: Teeth on edge)
Sheep to the slaughter
  (See: Led as a sheep to the slaughter)
Sheep's clothing
  (See: Wolf in sheep's clothing)
Sowing and reaping
  (See: You reap what you sow)
Swords into plowshares
  (See: Beat swords into ploughshares)
Take you under my wing(s)
  (See: Under my wings)
Teeth on edge
  (See: Sour grapes)
The mighty are fallen
  (See: How are the mighty fallen)
There's nothing new under the sun
  (See: Nothing new under the sun)
Thorn in my side
  (See: Thorn in the flesh)
Time and a place for everything
  (See: To everything there is a season)
Twinkling of an Eye
  (See: In the twinkling of an eye)
Weighed in the balance
  (See: Writing on the wall)
Wit's End

(See: At wits' end)
Wolves in Sheep's Clothing
(See: Wolf in sheep's clothing)
Ye of little faith
(See: O ye of little faith)

Other Phrases

The following phrases or expressions come from the Bible but for one or more reasons they are not included in the main listings with source verse, definition and examples.

Some of these other phrases are used exclusively in religious communities. The purpose of this book is to describe phrases in more general use. Many of these expressions are almost always quoted as Bible verses rather than used naturally in a sentence. Our purpose in this book was not to identify verses of scripture that people—even some who are not part of a religious community—are familiar with and/or can quote. Rather, we were interested in phrases that are occasionally or even routinely employed for their value as idioms, similes, metaphors or figures of speech in conversation or writing.

A few of these phrases might be argued by some either not to come from the Bible more than from some other source, or to have shaky credit to the scriptures.

Still other phrases are used only as titles, or are of such insignificant occurrence in everyday language that they didn't merit treatment in the main listings.

The scripture shown as the source of any one of these phrases may be, and in many cases is, only one of several verses containing the phrase.

Blessed are the peacemakers - Matthew 5:9
Breath of life - Genesis 2:7
Burning the midnight oil - Matthew 25:6-8)
By their fruits ye shall know them - Matthew 7:16-21
By the rivers of Babylon - Psalm 137
Chariots of Fire - 2 Kings 6:17
Do unto others - Matthew 7:12
Don't lose heart - 2 Corinthians 4:16
Doubting Thomas - John 20:24-29

Everything under the sun - Ecclesiastes 1:3

Flesh and blood - Ephesians 6:2

From strength to strength - Psalm 84:7

Fruit of your loins - Genesis 35:11

Garden of Eden - Genesis 2:10

Get thee behind me - Matthew 4:10

God save the king - 1 Samuel 10:24

Good news - Matthew 4:23

Good things come to those that wait - Lamentations 3:25

Graven image - Exodus 20:4

Half was not told me - 1 Kings 10:7

Have you in my heart - Philippians 1:7

Heart's desire - Psalm 37:4

Heavens above - Isaiah 45:8

Heavy heart - Proverbs 25:20

Honor thy father and mother - Exodus 20:12

Howling wilderness - Deuteronomy 32:10

Inherit the wind - Proverbs 11:29

Iron sharpens iron - Proverbs 27:17

Keys of the kingdom - Matthew 16:19

King of Kings - Revelation 19:16

Land of Nod - Genesis 4:16

Let my people go - Exodus 7:16

Lilies of the field - Matthew 6:28

Lion's den - Daniel 6

Love covers a multitude of sins - James 5:20

Love thy neighbor as thyself - Mark 12:31

Lovingkindness - Psalm 32:10

Many are called but few are chosen - Matthew 22:14

More than heart could wish - Psalm 73:7

Morning star - Job 38:7

My heart's desire - Romans 10:1

My name is legion - Mark 5:9

My rock - Psalm 19:14

New wine into old bottles - Luke 5:38

Old as Methuselah - Genesis 5:27
Pillars of the earth - Job 9:6
Power and the glory - 1 Chronicles 29:11
Practice what you preach - Romans 2:21
Prepare to meet your God - Amos 4:12
Rest in peace - Isaiah 57:2
Separate the wheat from the chaff - Matthew 3:12
Shiloh - Jeremiah 41:5
Showers of blessing - Ezekiel 34:26
Sleeping the sleep of the righteous - Proverbs 3:24
Snow in summer - Proverbs 26:1
Soft answer turns away wrath - Proverbs 15:1
Spy out the land - Numbers 13:1-2
Storm and tempest - Isaiah 29:6
Strength to strength - Psalm 84:7
Take root - Isaiah 27:6
Ten commandments - Deuteronomy 4:13
Thank God - Romans 7:25
Thanksgiving - Leviticus 7:15
Thou shalt not kill - Exodus 20:13
Thou shalt not bear false witness - Exodus 20:16
Three score and ten - Psalm 90:10
Tree of life - Genesis 2:9
Truth shall make you free - John 8:37
Turned the world upside down - Acts 17:6
Voice crying in the wilderness - John 1:23
Way of all the earth - 1 Kings 2:2
What God has joined together - Matthew 19:6
Wheel within a wheel - Ezekiel 1:16
White as snow - Isaiah 1:18
World without end - Ephesians 3:21
You don't know the half of it - 1 Kings 10:7

www.ingramcontent.com/pod-product-compliance
Lightning Source LLC
Chambersburg PA
CBHW030415100426
42812CB00028B/2972/J